Sue,
The re[illegible]
relationship [illegible]
on the cover o[illegible]
Cheers!!

Sex & Spaghetti

"It's All You Think About!"

by Nick Bartlone

ISBN-10: 0615700454

EAN-13: 9780615700458

For my Grandmothers:

Josephine Notareschi

and

Rose Bartlone

For making every meal a feast and every family gathering a celebration.

(I hope they forgive me for the title!)

"Cookery is not chemistry. It is an art. It requires instinct and taste rather than exact measurements."

Chef Marcel Boulestin

ACKNOWLEDGEMENTS

I would like to thank my entire family, especially my Mom (my biggest fan) and my friends, for their encouragement and support in my pursuit of my writing Sex & Spaghetti. *Let's face it. A retired Marine? Writing a cookbook? It's a stretch!!*

I would like to thank the following people for their contributions to Sex & Spaghetti: *Anna, Popo, Uncle Buck & Aunt Kathy Notareschi, Sok & Jeni Verdery, Uncle Sonny & Aunt Gwen Bartlone, Georgie Martinko (my mother-in-law), Nib, Cousin Jodi Julian, Jill Dunyon, Carrie Chong, Russ & Jess Kaniho, Lauren & Nicole LaVine, Marybeth Seiple, Sandy Montalvo, Giovanni & Lucia Lucignano, Jen Storm, and Patricia Taitano. Some provided recipes, some inspired recipes, and others had the arduous duty of taste-testing recipes. They all have a love of food and a deep understanding of the importance it has in bringing people together, and for that I thank them.*

I would also like to thank Hope LaVine for editing my work, and Gina Keeley for making the most out of my photography.

Finally, I would like thank Sher, my wife, for encouraging me to write Sex & Spaghetti. *She once claimed, "It's all you think about!"*

"Food without wine is a corpse; wine without good food is a ghost; united and well matched they are as body and soul, living partners."

ANDRE SIMON

CONTENTS

The recipes in *Sex & Spaghetti* are arranged according to people, places, and events.

Within the chapters the recipes are listed alphabetically. Recipes with the (30<) symbol can be prepared in 30 minutes or less.

INTRODUCTION

I believe that people act in one of two ways when using a cookbook. There are those who will follow a recipe to the letter, measuring everything exactly, and cooking the ingredients not one second longer than the recipe states, believing that the recipe is perfect as-is. Then there are those who are sceptical of the recipe before they even start to make it. They think, "I could make this better. That's not enough salt. You need to cook it longer than that. And that's not the way Momma used to make it!"

I think that they all have the right approach because they want their meals to be something special. They want to cook something that they can share with family and friends. And when family and friends gather around great food, special moments are made. This, my fellow cooks, chefs, and grill-masters, is what Sex & Spaghetti is all about.

Over the past 25 years I have had the honor and privilege of serving in the United States Marine Corps. During those 25 years I had the good fortune of being sent to great duty stations such as Guam and Hawai'i; Naples, Italy; and Yuma, Arizona, to name a few. And while all of those locations offered exciting activities and beautiful sights, the relationships that I formed are what I most cherish today.

Don't get me wrong, I love food, and have been known to drive hours across Arizona just for my favorite fish tacos on 16th Street in Yuma. When I visit Hawai'i I eat my way around O'ahu – that's exhausting. Naples, Italy? Don't get me started!

But let me be clear when I say that food is only food, no matter how good, unless it is shared with others. I am confident that the most recent great meal that you ate was memorable because of those with whom you shared it.

I hope you enjoy trying the recipes within Sex & Spaghetti, *and I also hope that many great memories, with friends and family, are made in the process.*

"Dining with one's friends and beloved family is certainly one of life's primal and most innocent delights. One that is both soul-satisfying and eternal."

Julia Child

VINO & BEER: RULES & RECOMMENDATIONS

I talk a lot about adult beverages in this book, so I think I need to lay down some ground rules which will, hopefully, guarantee a more enjoyable experience.

Rule #1: DO NOT DRINK AND DRIVE.........period.

–A little planning can go a long way.

–Volunteer to drive: You'll get your turn behind the glass.

Rule #2: A Red Solo cup has its purposes; drinking wine out of it is not one of them!

–Beer works a little better from these cups, especially if it's from a keg and you have no other receptacle except a beer bong to drink from.

Rule #3: Avoid the hangover.

–One drink. One glass of water. One drink. One glass of water. One drink,......... This may be the most useful recipe that I give you!

–Another option is to just drink a little less.

Rule #4: White with fish. Red with meat.

-I am not trying to put you in a box; however, if you have yet to figure out what you like, this is a good rule to follow.

Rule #5: Beer is good with more than just chips.

-Like wine, certain beers will pair better with certain foods.

-BEER! The hottest foods don't fare well with wine!

-Cold beer is usually my favorite brand, but it is fun to experiment.

Rule #6: Refer to Rule #1

Vino & Beer Recommendations

Here are some recommendations that may help you pair your food with your drink. This list is not all-inclusive, but it is offered as a guide; you should experiment, as your taste may differ. Palates are like opinions; we all have one, and each is unique.

WINE

LIGHT BODY

Pinot Noir

Very versatile: Mushrooms; potatoes; duck and goose; salmon; tuna; lamb; venison; roast beef; butter sauces; spicy dishes.

Pinot Grigio

Pork; chicken; Alfredo sauces; bratwurst; light fish; oysters; light pasta; citrus fruits.

Riesling

Versatile: Great for an appetizer table; also for hot-and-spicy dishes. Chinese; fried chicken; bratwurst; sushi; crab.

Sauvignon Blanc

Extra-sharp Cheddar; Pecorino; shrimp; lobster; oysters; clams; sushi; delicate white fish such as cod or sole; asparagus; pork; chicken.

MEDIUM BODY

Merlot

Cheddar and mild yellow cheeses; roasted or baked chicken; pork roast; mushrooms.

Syrah

Roast beef or steak; barbecued ribs; grilled meat; wild game.

Zinfandel

Hard cheeses; meats; poultry; hamburgers; barbecue; tomato-based dishes; chili; pizza.

HEAVY BODY

Cabernet Sauvignon

Grilled, roasted, or braised red meat; chicken; duck; mushrooms; squash.

Malbec

Grilled, roasted, smoked or barbecued red meat and pork; chicken; smoked salmon.

Chardonnay

Cream sauces; chicken and turkey; pork; lobster; shrimp; sea bass; salmon; spinach; squash.

BEER

LIGHT BODY

Lager

Spicy food; shellfish; sushi; pork with; chicken, either grilled or roasted.

Pilsner

American and Monterey Jack cheeses; spicy food; salads; salmon; tuna.

Wheat/Hefeweizen

Feta cheese; light soups and salads; sushi; citrus-flavored desserts.

MEDIUM BODY

Ale

Cheddar, Parmigiano, and Romano cheeses; spicy food; burgers; buffalo wings; pizza.

IPA

Curry; buffalo wings; shrimp; crab.

Bock

Swiss cheese; Cajun food; jerk chicken; beef; sausage.

HEAVY BODY

Stout

Roasted, smoked, and barbecued foods; oysters; rich stews; chocolate. Try making pancakes with Stout.

Porter

Smoked foods; barbecue; sausage; meats; bacon; chili.

NOTES

****Here are a few things to keep in mind when using the following recipes:*

– When you see "Egg" just assume they are Large Eggs.

– "Butter" is always Unsalted Butter; it's easier to regulate the salt this way.

– Unless otherwise specified, "Flour" is always All-Purpose Flour.

– The wine and beer recommendations are exactly that – recommendations.

– And, last but not least, you're not always going to get specifics. In other words, sometimes you'll just have to experiment to see what you like best.

"After a good dinner one can forgive anybody, even one's own relatives."

Oscar Wilde

CHAPTER ONE

Family & Friends

My family kept to the basics, cooking with simple, fresh ingredients that were readily available. For the most part, the recipes within Sex & Spaghetti follow that same path.

The recipes within this Chapter are either old family recipes (mostly Italian), recipes from friends, or recipes developed from my experimenting.

Some of the Family: West Pittsburgh, Pennsylvania

Anise Seed Cookies (Biscotti)

Biscotti, or biscotti di Prato, means twice-baked biscuits, originating in the Italian city of Prato. This recipe comes from the Pennsylvanian city of Bessemer; it's like Prato, only better.

I've tried and tried to make these like my Mom does, but somehow they always fall short. Of course they never go to waste.

INGREDIENTS:

1 cup Sugar
8 Tbsp Butter (melted)
6 Eggs
3/4 tsp Salt
2–3 Tbsp Anise Seeds
1 tsp Vanilla
5 cups All-Purpose Flour
1 Tbsp Baking Powder

DIRECTIONS:

1. Preheat oven to 350 degrees.

2. Mix together Sugar, Butter, Eggs, Salt, Anise Seeds, and Vanilla.

3. Combine Flour and Baking Powder and add to above ingredients. Mix well.

4. Separate dough into four equal portions; then form four logs.

5. Place each log in a 9″ x 5″ loaf-shaped baking pan and flatten each until they are ½-inch in height, as the dough will double in size.

6. Place baking pans in oven and bake for approximately 25 minutes.

7. Remove pans from the oven and let loaves cool for about 15 minutes.

8. Remove loaves from pans and cut each into ½-inch slices.

9. On a cookie sheet, bake each biscotti on one side until they start to brown, about 10 minutes; then flip and bake until desired crispness.

10. Once cooled they will become very crisp and great for dunking in coffee, milk, or even wine. They're not so bad straight out of the oven either!

* Should make about 48 biscotti.

**There are many variations of biscotti. Experiment with other ingredients such as nuts, chocolate, and dried fruits, to discover your own favorites.

Baked Chicken or Pork Chops

This is a healthy, quick-and-simple recipe using either chicken or pork. I prefer boneless chicken breasts or thighs, but your favorite part of the chicken will work just fine. Adjust cooking times as necessary.

INGREDIENTS:

Chicken Pieces
Pork Chops
Italian Bread Crumbs
(I like VIGO or Progresso brands)
Olive Oil

DIRECTIONS:

1. Preheat oven to 350.
2. Cover the meat with Olive Oil and then a light coating of Bread Crumbs.
3. Place prepared meat on a non-stick baking sheet and place in oven.
4. Bake until juices run clear. For boneless chicken breasts, approximately 35 minutes, thighs about 25 minutes. For chops, depending upon their thickness, about 30 minutes.

*For a quick Chicken Parmigiano dish, top chicken with Mozzarella cheese and a heavy dose of "Nicky's Pasta Sauce" (see p. 28), and return to the oven until cheese melts. Sprinkle with Parmigiano cheese and serve with pasta.

**This dish is very wine-friendly, regardless of whether you make it with chicken or pork. A Merlot, a Chianti, or a Chardonnay will work well with either.

Big Nick's Sicilian Steak

Growing up, I thought that breading a steak, wrapping it in aluminum foil and putting it under the broiler was common, but I've since discovered that it is unique to the Sicilian side of my family.

INGREDIENTS:

Your favorite cut of Beef Steak
Olive Oil
Italian Breadcrumbs
(I like VIGO or Progresso brands)
Garlic
Aluminum Foil
Salt & Pepper

DIRECTIONS:

1. Turn on your oven's broiler.
2. Lightly coat steak with olive oil.
3. Cover steak with breadcrumbs.
4. Place steak on a piece of foil big enough to completely wrap the steak.
5. Cut chunks of garlic and place on top of steak.
6. Tightly seal the aluminum foil around the steak.
7. Place sealed steak under the broiler. A ½ inch steak should take approximately 40 minutes to completely cook.
8. Open your masterpiece carefully as it will be very hot inside the foil pouch. Return to broiler to let the steak brown a little—for no more than 5 minutes, or the steak will become dry.
9. Add salt and pepper as necessary. Serve hot with your favorite adult beverage.

*You could add many ingredients to this dish: Hot peppers, mushrooms and onions, etc., but this is the way that it was introduced to me.

Caponata Siciliana

I can't make this recipe without thinking of a friend from Hawai'i. Randy loves good food, and is willing to taste about anything. We had a gathering at the house and I made this recipe, wondering if it would go over with the guests. I figured that Randy would give me an honest answer, so I decided to ask him. As I approached, he turned around, with a mouth full of caponata, olive oil dripping down his chin, and sort of said, "This is good!" He made my night.

You can find many Caponata recipes, with many different ingredients and preparation methods. What you see below is my version. Add, subtract, or adjust ingredients as you see fit. The beauty of this recipe is that you will quickly make it your own, and it will be wonderful. Don't like zucchini, but love fennel? Do it!

This very versatile Sicilian favorite is good warm or cold. Eat with a crusty bread, on a sandwich, or on a pizza. I've not tried mixing it with pasta, but I can't imagine that it would be anything but incredible. I'm thinking gnocchi.

Caponata

INGREDIENTS:

1 medium Eggplant, firm (unpeeled, cut in small chunks)
3 Tbsp Salt
¼ cup Olive Oil
2 cloves Garlic (minced)
¼ cup Sweet Onion (diced)
½ cup Green Sicilian Olives (quartered)
½ cup Calamata Olives (quartered)
1 jar Capers (3.5 oz, drained)
2-3 small Zucchini (cut in small chunks)
1 Roasted Red Pepper (coarsely chopped)
(See "Roasted Pepper" recipe, p. 33)
2 celery ribs, chopped
½ cup Golden Raisins
1 can Crushed Tomatoes (28 oz)
3 large Basil leaves (chopped)
½ tsp dried Oregano
½ tsp each, Salt & Black Pepper

DIRECTIONS:

1. I've seen this recipe made in about four different pans, but I'm not interested in that kind of clean-up; so we're going to cook in just one. A deep 12-inch frying pan should do the trick.

2. Cut Eggplant into eatable-sized chunks; then soak in salted water. This step will help rid the eggplant of bitterness. After 30 minutes remove the eggplant from salted water, rinse, and drain in colander.

3. While eggplant is soaking, prepare other vegetables per above ingredients list.

4. Heat the Olive Oil, and add Garlic, Onion, Capers, and Olives, and sauté´ for a couple of minutes over medium heat. Add Celery, Zucchini, Roasted Red Pepper, Raisins, and Eggplant, and cook for another couple of minutes; then add Tomatoes and cook for approximately 20 minutes or until eggplant is tender. Mixture will cook down considerably, so don't worry that your pan is overflowing to start with.

5. Add Basil, Sugar, Oregano, and Salt and Pepper, and cook for one minute.

6. Serve warm or cold.

**I like a dry white wine with this dish. Try your favorite Pinot Grigio.

Citrus-Smoked Chicken

This could be the juiciest chicken that you'll ever eat.

Soaking the chicken in a brine prior to cooking adds flavor and tenderness to the meat.

This recipe brings back great memories from South Carolina, Georgia, and, especially, Hawai'i, where I dragged my smoker to the beach on more than one occasion.

Thank you, Uncle Buck!

Smoked Chicken and Ribs: Kaneohe Bay, Hawai'i

INGREDIENTS:

1 Chicken (whole)
1 can Orange Juice Concentrate
1 gallon Water
1 cup Salt
2 Oranges, quartered
2 Lemons, quartered
½ lb Oak or Fruit Wood Chips

DIRECTIONS:

1. Place the Whole Chicken (insides removed) in a large pot or large zip-lock storage bag.

2. Mix Orange Juice Concentrate with water.

3. Add Salt to orange juice and mix well to make a brine.

4. Pour this orange juice brine over chicken, ensuring chicken is completely covered with liquid; and put it in refrigerator.

5. Brine chicken for 12 hours.

6. Soak wood chips in water for at least 30 minutes.

7. Preheat your smoker or grill to 225 degrees.

8. Remove chicken from brine and stuff with Orange and Lemon chunks.

9. Remove wood chips from water; place them in smoke box; then put in smoker or on grill. If using a grill, also have a

full bowl of water, or some liquid (beer or juice) inside the grill.

10. Place chicken in smoker or on grill and allow to smoke and cook for approximately 5 hours, checking the internal temperature of the chicken (the breast meat) around the 4-hour mark. After the first hour the smoking should stop. Ensure you keep liquid in the bowl the entire cooking time.

11. Once the internal temperature of the chicken (breast meat) has reached 170 degrees, remove chicken from heat and let rest for 15 minutes before serving.

*For a more savory dish, substitute plain water for orange juice; and stuff the chicken with garlic and fresh rosemary instead of fruit.

**Zinfandel or an Australian Shiraz always goes well at a barbecue.

Cream Puffs

INGREDIENTS:

Pudding

2 pks (3.4 oz) Instant French Vanilla Pudding Mix
2 cups Heavy Cream
1 cup Milk

Puffs

1 cup Water
½ cup Butter
1 tsp Sugar
2 cups Flour
½ tsp Salt
4 Eggs

Chocolate Sauce

¾ cup Heavy Cream
1 Tbsp Butter
6 oz Bittersweet Chocolate (chopped)

DIRECTIONS:

1. Preheat oven to 425 degrees.

2. Prepare pudding by combining Pudding Mix, Heavy Cream, and Milk. Cover and refrigerate.

3. In a medium saucepan bring Water, Butter, and Sugar to a boil. Remove from heat.

4. Stir in Flour and Salt with a wooden spoon until mixture pulls away from sides of pan. Let cool.

5. Add Eggs one at a time, mixing after each, stirring until batter comes together.

6. If you do not have a pastry bag, and would rather not use a spoon, transfer batter to a large zip-top bag. With batter in one corner of bag, snip a ½-inch opening in the opposite corner.

7. Line a baking sheet with parchment paper.

8. Squeeze desired amount of batter onto baking sheet (2 tablespoons will make a large puff.)

9. Bake for 10 minutes at 425 degrees; then reduce oven temp to 350 and bake until puffs are golden brown, about 20 – 30 minutes.

10. Let cool on baking sheet.

11. Once cool, cut off top third of each puff and scoop out the soft dough in center.

12. Spoon or use pastry bag to fill with pudding. Replace tops.

FOR CHOCOLATE SAUCE:

1. Combine Heavy Cream and Butter in a small sauce pan and bring to a boil.
2. Remove from heat and add Chocolate.
3. Once chocolate is melted, whisk until smooth.
4. Drizzle Chocolate Sauce over Cream Puffs.

Fresh Ricotta Cheese

Once you taste fresh Ricotta you will not want the store-bought kind.

Trust me; it is much easier to make than you would think.

There are a number of recipes within this book that using fresh Ricotta will make extra special.

INGREDIENTS:

2 quarts Whole Milk
1 cup Heavy Cream
3 Tbsp White Vinegar
½ tsp Salt
***Cheesecloth*

DIRECTIONS:

1. In a medium sauce pan, warm the Milk and Cream until the temperature reaches 185 degrees, and the surface gets foamy. <u>It's important that the mixture doesn't boil.</u>

2. Remove from heat, add Vinegar, and stir. The mixture will curdle.

3. Add the Salt and gently stir for another minute.

4. Cover the pot with a towel and leave at room temperature for 2 hours.

5. Set a large colander in a bowl. Line the colander with cheesecloth.

6. Once you remove the towel from the pot, you will see the cheese curd floating. Remove the curd from the pot with a slotted spoon and place in the lined colander.

7. Gather the corners of the cheesecloth and close with a rubber band. You should have a softball-sized ball of cheese. After 30 minutes squeeze some of the whey out of the cheese, adjusting the rubber band so that the ball becomes smaller. Repeat this process twice more.

8. Remove fresh Ricotta from cheesecloth and use immediately. Fresh ricotta can also be refrigerated for up to four days, but it is best when used fresh.

*Makes about 3 cups of ricotta.

**Cheesecloth is a loose-woven cotton cloth used primarily for making cheese. In some styles of cheese-making it is used to remove whey from the cheese curd and helps hold the curds together as the cheese is formed. Cheesecloth is also used for making custards, tofu, and yogurt, and for straining soup stock. You can find cheesecloth in most grocery stores and such places as Walmart.

*** If we're getting technical, Ricotta is not a cheese, but a cheese by-product. Ricotta is made from the whey that is drained from the curds once the cheese is made. This doesn't mean that you cannot make it from milk, but the traditional method is to make it from whey, especially that of Mozzarella.

Georgie's Rice & Sausage Casserole

A party in the Martinko Family Basement isn't a party without this dish.

This casserole is really meant to be a side dish; however, I can make a meal out of it; and I have.

INGREDIENTS:

½ lb Sweet Italian Sausage (casings removed)
½ lb Hot Italian Sausage (casings removed)
½ stick Butter
½ cup chopped Mushrooms
½ cup Onion
4-½ cups Water
1 cup White Rice
2 pkgs Lipton's Chicken Noodle Soup

DIRECTIONS:

1. Brown the Sausage in medium frying pan, breaking it into small pieces.
2. Drain sausage and discard oil. Set sausage aside.
3. In the same pan, melt the Butter. Add Vegetables and sauté´until soft.

4. In a large pot, boil Water and add the Soup packages and Rice. Cook for approximately 25 minutes or until rice is tender and all water has been absorbed.

5. Add sausage and vegetables to pot and mix well.

6. Serve warm.

Jill's Monster Meatballs and Marinara

This recipe is further proof that I am surrounded by great cooks.

These Meatballs are an experience. They are the size of a baseball with a stadium size flavor to match. Just watching them fry in the pan makes me happy!

MEATBALL INGREDIENTS:

½ cup Chicken Broth
¼ cup coarsely chopped Yellow Onion
1 clove Garlic
1 lb ground Beef
1 lb ground Pork
4 Eggs, beaten
1 cup Bread Crumbs
1/3 cup chopped Italian Flat-Leaf Parsley
½ cup Grated Parmigiano
1 tsp Crushed Red Pepper
¼ cup Olive Oil

DIRECTIONS:

1. Combine Chicken Broth, Onion and Garlic in food processor and puree.
2. In large bowl combine this mixture with all remaining ingredients.
3. Form the Meatballs the size of a baseball.

4. Cook in hot Oil over medium heat to sear meat and seal in flavor.

5. The Meatballs do not need to cook through. They will finish cooking after dropped in marinara where they should simmer for at least 1 hour.

MARINARA INGREDIENTS:

½ cup finely chopped Yellow Onion
3 cloves Garlic
3 tbsp Olive Oil
48 oz Tomato Puree
28 oz Crushed Tomatoes
2 tbsp Tomato Paste
2 ½ cups Water
1 cup Chicken Broth
1 tsp Sugar
½ tsp Crushed Red Pepper

DIRECTIONS:

1. Over medium heat, cook garlic and onion in skillet with olive oil until soft, but not brown.

2. In a large pot add Tomato Puree and Crushed Tomatoes. Add ingredients from skillet.

3. Stir in remaining ingredients. Bring to boil then reduce heat to simmer, cooking for at least 1 hour. The longer it cooks the thicker and more flavorful it will become.

Lemon Ricotta Cheese Cake

I love lemon! I took my Mom's recipe for this cheese cake; then I added lemon instead of the cinnamon that her recipe called for. You can't beat this, with a cup of coffee, for breakfast.

INGREDIENTS:

Filling

32 oz Ricotta
2 Eggs
1 tsp Lemon Oil
1 tsp Vanilla
½ cup Sugar
½ tsp Salt

DIRECTIONS:

1. Mix all ingredients well.
2. Refrigerate until you are ready to fill pie crust.

GEORGIE'S PIE CRUST

1 cup All-Purpose Flour (sifted)
½ tsp Salt
¼ cup plus 1 Tbsp Crisco Shortening
2 Tbsp Milk

1. Mix all ingredients with fork until all flour is moistened. Form dough into a ball. Put dough between two pieces of waxed paper and roll flat.

2. Although I make a pie crust, I like to use a cake pan for baking this crust because, well, this is a cake! The tricky part—for me at least—is getting the crust centered in the pan so that it cooks evenly (good luck with that). Poke holes in the dough with a fork before baking.

3. Bake at 475 for 8–10 min or until starting to brown.

4. Once the crust is cooked and cooled, pour well-mixed filling into cake pan and bake at 350 for about 60 minutes. Tooth pick should come out clean. Allow to cool completely on wire rack. Cheesecake will continue to cook as it cools.

*I like to serve this cold, from the refrigerator, but room temp is also great.

Nib's Gnocchi

Making good gnocchi takes patience and practice. One of the best plates of gnocchi that I've ever eaten was made by a friend who seems to have the process down to a science. Below is Nib's recipe with a few tips to help you make some melt-in-your-mouth gnocchi.

INGREDIENTS:

8 Medium Russet Potatoes
4 cups Flour
Egg Beaters (one container) or 3 eggs

DIRECTIONS:

1. Bake the Potatoes until soft.
2. Once cooked, cut in half, lengthwise, and let them cool for 10–15 minutes.
3. Once cooled, peel; then rice the potatoes* in a large bowl. **Do not use 'mashed' potatoes.**
4. Add 3 cups of the Flour, the Egg Beaters (or 3 Eggs), and mix together. The dough should have enough flour so that it is not sticky; too much flour and the gnocchi will come out too hard. There is only one way to figure out the right consistency, and that is to practice.
5. Once the dough is mixed, cut off a piece and roll it out into a rope about 1 inch in diameter.

6. Cut into ½-inch pieces.

7. Continue with that process until you've used all of your dough.

8. Gently boil in salted water until the gnocchi float to the surface.

9. Drain water and serve with your favorite sauce.

*Potato Ricers can be found in most department stores and online.

**Makes about 5 lbs of pasta.

*** For a white sauce, try combining the following: ½ cup Butter, ½ cup Parmigiano, ¼ tsp Nutmeg, and ¾ tsp Ground Sage. Simmer all ingredients for 10 minutes in small sauce pan; then pour over fresh gnocchi.

Nicky's Pasta Sauce

I rarely make a pot of sauce exactly the same twice; so before writing down the ingredients below, I had to make a pot of sauce and actually measure things; but, I usually taste and adjust as I go along.

The good news is that I think you are going to like the following recipe; it is easy to make and gets better the longer you let it cook.

INGREDIENTS:

1-2 Tbsp Olive Oil
2 cloves Garlic (chopped)
1 (6 oz) can Tomato Paste
5 cans Tomato Sauce (15 oz)
2 ½ cups Water
½–1 tsp Salt
½–1 tsp Black Pepper
½ tsp Crushed Red Pepper (optional)
½ tsp Fennel Seeds (optional)
Sicilian Meatballs, recipe p. 35 and/or
Italian Sausage, p. 77

DIRECTIONS:

1. Heat Olive Oil over medium heat and add Garlic. Cook for 1 minute.

2. Add Tomato Sauce, Tomato Paste, and Water. Stir.

3. Add ½ tsp Salt and ½ tsp Black Pepper and stir.

4. Bring sauce to a slow boil, stirring occasionally.
5. While sauce is cooking, prepare the Meatballs and/or Sausage.
6. Once meat is cooked, add it to sauce.
7. After a couple of hours taste the sauce, and add Salt and Pepper according to your taste.
8. Cook for at least 5 hours, stirring approximately every 30 minutes. Sauce should thicken as it cooks.
9. Serve over pasta or just dip bread in it. You're gonna love this easy-to-make sauce!

*If I have hot sausage in the recipe, I won't add the red pepper or fennel to the sauce; but without hot sausage, I will include the fennel seeds and red pepper.

Pumpkin Cheesecake

I was excited to take this cheesecake to a Thanksgiving dinner at my Aunt and Uncle's house in Myrtle Beach. It had been a busier-than-usual week, but I managed to get the cake made, and began the two-hour drive to their house. About 45 minutes into the trip I realized that I had forgotten the cheesecake. Having put so much work into it, I decided to return home for the cake, even though it made me late for dinner. But I was bringing dessert, so I was quickly forgiven.

Dinner was spectacular, with lots of family and friends, surrounded by great food and wine, and with lots of laughs. And now for dessert!

I was particularly proud of my cheesecake: It looked great, and everyone was excited for a taste; and it must be good, considering what it took to get it to the table.

Much to my surprise and embarrassment, the cake was awful. Everyone was complimenting me but, although no one said it, I knew they were thinking: Bless his heart!

If you are going to make this cheesecake, do not, I repeat, DO NOT forget the sugar. Even with all of the other great tasting ingredients, without the sugar, your cake is sure to find its way to the trashcan.

INGREDIENTS:

¾ cup Gingersnaps (crushed)
½ cup Almonds *(*toasted, then ground)*
½ cup Butter (melted)
3 packages Cream Cheese (8 oz each)
½ cup Sugar

½ cup Brown Sugar (packed)
2 Tbsp Milk
4 Eggs
1 ½ cups canned Pumpkin
¼ cup Sour Cream
2 Tbsp Ground Cinnamon
½ tsp Ground Ginger
½ tsp Ground Cardamom
¼ tsp Ground Cloves

DIRECTIONS:

1. Heat oven to 375 degrees.
2. Combine the Gingersnaps, Almonds, and Butter for the crust.

*(*To toast almonds, put them on a baking sheet, in the oven, for just a few minutes on each side. Do not allow to burn.)*

3. Press crust mixture onto the bottom and about an inch up the sides of a 9" Springform pan.
4. In a large bowl, beat the Cream Cheese, both Sugars, and Milk until combined.
5. Slowly mix in the Eggs (at low speed) until just combined with above mixture.
6. Add the remaining ingredients—Pumpkin, Sour Cream, Cinnamon, Ginger, Cardamom, and Cloves—and stir.
7. Pour this mixture on top of the crust.

8. Bake for approximately 60 minutes or until the center of the cake looks almost set and a toothpick comes out clean.

9. Cool on wire rack for 15 minutes; then loosen the crust from the sides of pan, but do not remove sides yet.

10. After 20 more minutes, remove the sides of the pan, and let the cake completely cool before moving to the refrigerator.

11. After four hours in the refrigerator, your Pumpkin Cheesecake is ready to serve.

Roasted Peppers

Roasted peppers can be used on sandwiches, and on pizzas, and in my "Caponatta" recipe, just to name a few ways. Roasted peppers bought in the store are often good, but there is nothing like making your own, especially since it's relatively simple to do.

INGREDIENTS:

Red Bell Peppers
Olive Oil
Garlic Salt

DIRECTIONS:

1. Preheat broiler.
2. Cut the Peppers in half. Remove seeds.
3. Coat peppers, inside and out, with Olive Oil.
4. Sprinkle peppers, inside and out, with Garlic Salt
5. On a non-stick baking sheet, put peppers, skin-side up, under the broiler.
6. Skin should start to bubble and blacken (about 12-15 minutes).
7. Remove from oven and place in a paper bag.

8. Close the bag and let peppers cool. This will help you remove the skins.

9. Once cooled, peel the skin off of the peppers.

10. Season with more garlic salt or fresh garlic, salt and pepper, and olive oil.

*If you plan to store the peppers, I recommend placing them in a sealed container with a heavy dose of olive oil; they will freeze well. I've tasted the peppers stored in vinegar, but I prefer them in oil.

Sicilian Meatballs

This meatball recipe has been in the works for many years. It combines the best of what I have learned from friends and family. The part I love about making meatballs is getting to taste-test, especially early on a Sunday morning!

INGREDIENTS:

1 lb Ground Beef
1 lb Ground Pork
2 Eggs
½ cup Parmigiano
½ cup low-sodium Chicken Broth
1 tsp Garlic (minced)
½ cup Italian Bread Crumbs
1–2 tsp Salt
½ tsp Black Pepper

DIRECTIONS:

1. Mix all ingredients thoroughly. Mixture should be wet, yet meatballs shouldn't break apart during cooking. If too dry, add more Chicken Broth.

2. Make a small patty and fry until cooked. Taste to see if you need to add anything, i.e., more Salt, Black Pepper, Garlic, etc. Of course this is also a great excuse to break out some fresh bread and have a mid-morning snack.

3. When you are happy with the test results, then form your meatballs and fry or bake until cooked. I'll sometimes do both; first searing them in a frying pan, then baking.

4. Once cooked, add meatballs to sauce and enjoy the aroma.

Shrimp Boil

Don't let that turkey cooker just sit there until Thanksgiving; put it to use by throwing a Shrimp Boil.

This is a great way to feed a lot of people at once and have minimal clean-up.

Hubert, North Carolina: Shrimp Boil

INGREDIENTS:

4 lbs Shrimp (shell/tail on)
2 dozen Ears of Corn (fresh, if possible, and halved)
3 lbs Small Red Potatoes

5 lbs Smoked Sausage
(pre-cooked Kielbasa, for instance, as hot as you like)
1 bag Old Bay Seasoning
1 Lemon (halved)
½ medium Onion
2 cloves Garlic (diced)
"Sok's Cocktail Sauce" (See recipe on page 40)
Butter (squeezable)
Salt &Pepper

DIRECTIONS:

1. Fill turkey cooker half-way with water and bring to a boil.

2. Add Old Bay Seasoning Bag, Onion, and Garlic.

3. While you are waiting for the water to boil, cover a table with newspapers, plastic, disposable tablecloth, or freezer paper.

4. Once water starts to boil, add the ingredients that will take longest to cook. In this case you're going to add the Potatoes. And although it's been previously cooked, add the Sausage, because it will give flavor to the potatoes. Return to a slow boil. Note: If you're using fresh corn, then you'll probably want to add this now also. If corn is frozen you should wait until later in the process.

5. Once potatoes are almost completely cooked, add the Frozen Corn, and return to slow boil; cook for 10 minutes.

6. Add fresh or frozen Shrimp and lemon (squeezing lemon juice into the pot first); cook for approximately 3 minutes or until shrimp turn pink; try not to over-cook.

7. It is best if you have a pot with a spigot at the bottom, but if not, drain the liquid from the pot carefully: It will be very hot!

8. Pour the drained contents of the pot onto the table.

9. Invite your guests to stand around the table and eat, or you can be a bit more civilized and use plates: No rules!

*Cold beer is a must for this occasion. Gotta have wine? Try a Pinot Noir, or a Viognier if you're feeling adventurous. Sauvignon Blanc would also do the trick.

**Crabs, oysters, clams, and mussels can be added.

Sok's Cocktail Sauce

When our family has a shrimp boil, I look forward to the cocktail sauce that my cousin Sok makes: It adds a little extra kick.

Recently I e-mailed Sok, asking for the recipe, and this what I received:

"Ketchup, little Worcestershire sauce, spoonful of horseradish, squeeze of lemon, and a vigorous shake of Texas Pete! Be sure to measure carefully!!"

Enjoy experimenting with these ingredients.

Emerald Isle, N.C., 2011: Shrimp/Crab Boil with my "little" cousin Johnny.

Spinach Rolls

INGREDIENTS:

Pizza Dough
Frozen Spinach
Minced Garlic
Olive Oil
Salt & Black Pepper
Ricotta Cheese

DIRECTIONS:

1. You can make the spinach rolls any size that you like; however, when I don't have the time to make my own dough, I like to use Rhodes Frozen Dinner Rolls. These rolls make a perfect personal spinach roll.

2. Preheat oven to 450 degrees.

3. In a frying pan, sauté the Garlic, as much as you like, in the Olive Oil for about one minute. Do not over-cook.

4. Add the Spinach, and Salt and Pepper to taste, and then mix all ingredients well.

5. Cook for 10 minutes, turning mixture over frequently. It is important to remove as much liquid as possible from spinach. Remove from heat.

6. On a lightly floured surface, roll out your dough to approximately 1/8-inch thickness.

7. Put a thin coat of Ricotta Cheese and the cooked spinach on the rolled-out dough.

8. Roll the dough into a log.

9. Place on cookie sheet or pizza stone and cook for approximately 10 minutes.

10. Best served warm.

Tuna & Capers

This dish is tasty, quick, and healthy! The one problem I have with this recipe is that once I start eating it, I can't stop!

INGREDIENTS:

¾ cup Olive Oil
1 tsp Garlic (minced)
3.5 oz jar Capers (drained)
½ tsp Oregano
½ tsp Black Pepper
1 can Albacore Tuna (in water)
Grated Pecorino or Parmigiano to taste
1 lb Penne or Rotini Pasta

DIRECTIONS:

1. Cook Pasta.
2. While pasta is cooking, heat Olive Oil and add to it the Garlic, Capers, Pepper, and Oregano. Allow this to simmer for about 5 minutes.
3. Drain water from Tuna. Then break up Tuna as small as you'd like and add to cooked pasta. Pour oil mixture over pasta and tuna, and mix well.
4. Serve immediately with Grated Cheese such as Pecorino or Parmigiano.

*I like this dish with a Sauvignon Blanc.
**Calamata olives are a welcome addition.
***I've been told that more garlic works too.

"Desserts are like mistresses. They are bad for you. So if you are having one, you might as well have two."

—Chef Alain Ducasse

CHAPTER

TWO

'Elua – Hawai'i

We Italians are completely obsessed with good food, but after spending nine years in Hawai'i, I can tell you that we are not alone.

When we think of Hawai'i, we think of white sandy beaches and lush tropical forests, but we would be wrong not to recognize the amazing food of the Hawai'ian Islands.

Most of the following recipes are Hawai'ian, although some are simply part of remembered special times.

Winemaking in Honolulu

Ahi Poke

The word poke (poh-keh) means, in Hawai'ian, "to slice or cut crosswise into pieces." When the native Hawai'ians first started eating poke it was a simple mixture of raw fish, Hawai'ian sea salt, seaweed, and chopped kukui nuts.

Today you will find a wide selection of poke recipes with octopus, raw crab, cooked shrimp, clams, or smoked salmon, to name just a few options.

Ahi is Yellow Fin Tuna.

Ahi Poke is usually served as an appetizer.

INGREDIENTS:

4 cups (about 2 lbs) fresh Ahi, cubed
¼ cup Green Onion
2 Tbsp Sesame Oil
1 cup Shoyu (soy sauce)
1 Tbsp Sesame Seeds (toasted)
1 Tbsp Crushed Red Pepper
1 tsp Sea Salt
½ tsp Fresh Ginger (grated)

DIRECTIONS:

1. Mix all ingredients thoroughly.

2. Put in refrigerator for 2 hours.

*Serve chilled with cold beer.

**Eating raw fish can be dangerous. Ensure you get quality fish from a reputable fishmonger.

Carrie's "Easy Cook" Spareribs

Carrie, another wonderful friend from Hawai'i, introduced me to this recipe almost twenty years ago. These ribs truly are "Easy Cook" and are also guaranteed to have you coming back for more.

INGREDIENTS:

3 lbs Pork Spareribs (boneless ones work best)
4 cloves Garlic (quartered)
½ cup Cider Vinegar
½ cup Brown Sugar
½ cup Shoyu (soy sauce)
2 Tbsp Cornstarch
1 can Pineapple (chunks)
6 oz (12 Tbsp) Pineapple Juice
Salt and Pepper

DIRECTIONS:

1. In a large pot, bring all ingredients—except the Pineapple, Pineapple Juice, and Cornstarch—to a boil.
2. Simmer and stir occasionally.
3. Cook approximately one hour or until spareribs are tender.
4. Add Cornstarch to Pineapple Juice and cook gently, while stirring, until thickened.

5. Pour Pineapple chunks and thickened juice over spareribs and cook an additional 15 minutes.

6. Add Salt and Pepper to taste.

7. Serve over Steamed Rice and do the hula.

*This recipe is also great made in the crockpot. Adjust cooking times as necessary.

**I would recommend a Pinot Noir with this dish.

Coconut Slaw

A staple at most back-yard gatherings in Hawai'i, and a refreshing change from Coleslaw.

INGREDIENTS:

½ cup Coconut Milk
½ cup Mayonnaise or Miracle Whip
2 Tbsp White Balsamic Vinegar
1 bag Coleslaw Salad Blend (16 oz)
½ cup Coconut Flakes
½ cup Golden Raisins

DIRECTIONS:

1. Whisk together Coconut Milk, Mayo, and Vinegar.
2. Add Coleslaw, Coconut Flakes, and Raisins. Toss to coat.
3. Serve cold.

*Makes about 6 servings

Guava Chicken

I can't even think about Guava Chicken without missing the Islands, the beach, the sand bar, manapua, loco moco, and countless other places and things. Of course, I mostly miss all of my wonderful friends. Mahalo, Russ & Jess, for this unbelievable recipe!

INGREDIENTS:

½ cup Ketchup
½ cup Oyster Sauce
½ cup Shoyu (soy sauce)
1 Tbsp Five Spice
Several chunks of fresh Ginger and Garlic (smashed)
5 lbs Boneless Chicken Thighs
1 can Frozen Pink Guava Juice

DIRECTIONS:

1. Mix well all ingredients—except the Guava Juice and Chicken—in a large pot. (If you'd like, reserve a cupful of this marinade; use it to baste the chicken while it cooks.)
2. Add Chicken and mix well.
3. Remove the Frozen Juice from can. (Don't thaw or dilute it.) Set the chunk of frozen juice on top of chicken.
4. Put in refrigerator and marinate overnight. (I stir it a couple of times after juice has thawed.)

5. Grill.

**Serve over steamed rice with a cold Longboard Lager or Primo. Do the hula again.

Ono-licious!!

Hobo Dinner

I was introduced to the Hobo Dinner at the beach one night. To make a Hobo Dinner, people each create their own meal by putting the ingredients they choose into a foil pouch before putting it on the grill.

INGREDIENTS:

You will need enough of the following ingredients to feed the number of people at your gathering. This is a recommended ingredients list and is certainly not all-inclusive.

Smoked Sausage
Ground Beef
Shrimp
Potatoes
Zucchini
Onions
Peppers
Salt
Pepper
Beer
Aluminum Foil
Sharpie (permanent marker)

DIRECTIONS:

1. Cut Sausage and Veggies into bite-sized pieces, and put in separate bowls, if possible.

2. Take a 12-inch piece of aluminum foil and fold in half, and then seal two of the ends so that you have a pouch to put your ingredients into. You may consider doubling the foil so as not to lose your ingredients.

3. Have everyone fill a pouch with the meat and veggies that they want to eat.

4. Add seasonings, including a splash or two of beer. Seal tight.

5. Write your name on pouch with Sharpie so that no one steals your masterpiece.

6. Place on grill or fire-grate and cook for approximately 30 minutes, turning over once or twice. Cooking times will vary depending on level of heat and type and amount of food.

*Cold beer.

Kalua Pua'a (Roasted Pork)

If you've ever been to a Luau you probably have had some smokey, salty, shredded pork that was cooked in a Hawai'ian imu, (an underground steam oven heated by wood and lava rock). This is not to say that pork is the only food cooked in this fashion, because the Hawai'ians also use the imu to cook breadfruit, bananas, sweet potatoes, taro, chicken, and fish.

Because it isn't always possible to dig a pit in the backyard, or to find banana and ti leaves, I've learned an easier way to make this dish by using a crock pot.

INGREDIENTS:

1 Pork Butt (the biggest you can fit in your crock pot)
1 cup Red Sea Salt
1 tsp Black Pepper
2 Tbsp Liquid Smoke (mesquite)
2 shots Whiskey
2 cups Rice
1 head of Cabbage (chopped and boiled until soft)

DIRECTIONS:

1. Rub Pork Butt with generous amounts of Sea Salt and Pepper.

2. Place Pork Butt, fat side up, in crock pot.

3. Add water to the crock pot to a depth of a little more than half-way up the side of the Pork.

4. Add Liquid Smoke and Whiskey.

5. Cook on low for 12–14 hours.

6. Remove Pork Butt from crock pot and shred with a fork. Serve warm, atop the rice and the cabbage.

*Since this is a Hawai'ian dish, a cold lager, like Primo, comes to mind. Can't find Primo? Samuel Adams Lager works well.

**For a different twist, mix the smoked pork with your favorite barbecue sauce for a delicious pulled-pork sandwich.

Lauren's Poor Man's Jambalaya

Jambalaya has nothing to do with Hawai'i, other than that this specific recipe is a reminder of a great friend's retirement party. Lots of food, adult beverages, and music made for a great party.

INGREDIENTS:

2 lbs Andouille Sausage
(or smoked kielbasa) sliced into bite-size pieces
6 Celery Stalks, cut into ½-inch slices
2 medium Onions (diced)
8 cloves Garlic (finely chopped)
1 large Red Bell Pepper (coarsely diced)
3 cups Long Grain White Rice, uncooked
6 cups Stock (chicken, beef, or vegetable)
¼ pound Butter
1 tsp Dry Mustard
1 tsp Cumin
1 tsp Black Pepper
1 tsp White Pepper
1 tsp Cayenne Pepper
(½ tsp for crowd-friendly heat; 2 tsps for spice-lovers)
1 tsp Salt
½ tsp Oregano
½ tsp Thyme
2 Bay Leaves

DIRECTIONS:

1. Chop all Vegetables and set aside in a large bowl.

2. Combine all Spices—except Bay Leaves—into a small bowl; mix well, and set aside.

3. Place Stock and Bay Leaves into a large pot and heat on medium-high.

4. Melt Butter on high in large frying pan, add Sausage, and cook for approximately 5 minutes, stirring often. When Sausage begins to brown, add Spice mixture, stirring the sausage so that the spices are evenly distributed. When the sausage is turning dark brown on all edges, add the Rice (dry) to the sausage-spice mixture, and continue to cook for another 5–10 minutes, stirring often; the goal is for the rice to acquire a 'dirty' brown color.

5. By now the soup stock should be near boiling. Add the sausage, rice, and vegetables to the soup stock—be careful when transferring or you'll get a Jambalaya facial—and bring all to a boil. Reduce heat.

6. Simmer covered for 20 minutes.

7. Fluff and serve with a side of crusty French bread.

Soak the pan immediately: You'll thank me for this.

*This recipe screams for a cold beer, like Sam Adams or Octoberfest. Too heavy for you? How about a Rolling Rock? From the glass-lined tanks of old Latrobe? Okay, maybe some vino. Keep in mind that this is a spicy dish. If you have to have wine I would go with a Reisling.

Loco Moco (Lo-Cal Version)

In Hawai'i, the Loco Moco is the ultimate in high-calorie breakfast food: Two scoops of rice; one beef patty on top of the rice; and two fried eggs on top of beef patty; all to be covered with gravy. My mouth is watering as I'm typing this.

As much as I love the Loco Moco, especially after a long hike or an early morning surf session, I needed to come up with a version that was a little lower in calories: I'm no longer nineteen years old. Well, this version is lower in calories and fat, while still providing plenty of protein, fiber, and taste.

INGREDIENTS:

½ cup Steel-Cut Oats
2 Eggs
½ cup Extra Sharp Cheddar Cheese (shredded)
Salt and Black Pepper

DIRECTIONS:

1. Cook Oats according to directions on package.
2. Scramble or, as I prefer, fry the Eggs.
3. Sprinkle the Cheese over the top of the Oatmeal, then top with the Eggs. Add Salt and Pepper to taste.
4. Serve hot.

A picture of the real Loco Moco.

MB's Portuguese Bean Soup

INGREDIENTS:

½ lb Kidney Beans (dried)
2–3 Ham Hocks
2 lbs Hot Portuguese Sausage
1 can Tomato Sauce (8 oz)
2 large Baking Potatoes (cut into ¾-inch cubes)
1 Onion (sliced)
3 Carrots (sliced)
3 Celery Stalks (sliced)
3 Tbsp Parsley (minced)
1 clove Garlic (minced)
1 Tbsp Lemon Juice
½ head Cabbage, shredded (optional)
½ cup Macaroni, Small Elbow (optional)
1 bunch Watercress (chopped) (optional)
½ tsp Allspice
Salt & Black Pepper

DIRECTIONS:

1. Cover Kidney Beans with water and soak overnight. Drain water when ready to use.

2. In a large pot, cover Ham Hocks with water and cook for 90 minutes.

3. Remove Ham Hocks from water and shred meat.

4. Remove as much fat as possible from water.

5. Add Kidney Beans to liquid and cook for one hour at a slow boil.

6. While beans are cooking, cut Portuguese Sausage into ½-inch slices; then sauté in frying pan.

7. Add shredded meat and sausage to soup and cook for at least 10 minutes.

8. Add Tomato Sauce, Potatoes, Onion, Carrots, Celery, Parley, Garlic, and Lemon Juice to soup; and simmer until vegetables are tender.

9. Add Cabbage, Pasta, Watercress, and Allspice. Simmer for another 10 minutes or until Pasta is tender.

*Serves 10

Sandra's Arros Con Pollo

(Rice with Chicken)

INGREDIENTS:

1 whole Chicken
4 cubes Chicken Bouillon
½ packet *Sazon Goya
1 cup Cilantro (chopped)
½ Tomato (chopped)
1¼ cup Carrots (chopped)
1 large Green Pepper (chopped)
1 cup Celery (chopped)
1 Onion, medium (chopped)
1/2 cup Soy Sauce (Kikoman)
5 cups of Long Grain Rice

DIRECTIONS:

1. Cut Chicken into four parts.
2. Place chicken in large pot, cover with water, and bring to a boil.
3. Add Sazon Goya and Chicken Bouillon.

4. Put ¼ cup of the Cilantro, ¼ of the Onion, and all the Tomato in blender and puree. Add to pot with chicken.

5. Once the chicken is cooked, remove it from the pot, saving the broth.

6. Add broth to Rice and ¼ cup of the Carrots and cook according to instructions on Rice package. Usually it's two cups of liquid for one cup of rice.

7. In a large frying pan, sauté remaining veggies until tender. Place in large bowl.

8. Shred chicken, then sauté with 1 Tbsp of the Soy Sauce. Add to bowl with veggies and mix.

9. Begin incorporating Rice and remaining Soy Sauce into chicken-veggie mix. Do not cover because that will make the rice mushy.

10. Serve hot with your favorite salsa.

*Goya products can be found in the specialty section of most grocery stores.

**A cold lager is what I like with this dish. I'm thinking Dos Equis: The green bottle.

"The Italians were eating with forks when the French were still eating each other."

—Mario Batali

CHAPTER THREE

Tre – Italy

Living in Italy was a dream come true. The sights, the sounds, the FOOD! We once sat around a table, fresh fava beans piled high in the middle, shucking them for hours: Shuck two, eat one. Plenty of cheese, bread, and wine to accompany the beans. Such a simple exercise that created so many great memories.

Having the opportunity to learn about my heritage while living in Italy was priceless. I was inside the house where my Grandfather was born. Saw the Pope. Walked the streets of Pompeii. My command of the Italian language? Let's just say that I could get us a great meal. Of course we'd probably get lost on our way to the ristorante, but I guess that would have been part of the adventure.

The meal photo below is only a glimpse of the great times, and unbelievable food, that I experienced while living in Italy. The recipes that follow are there because they remind me of special people, special times, and special places.

Another great meal with La Familia di Lucignano

Butternut Squash Risotto

Great risotto, prepared with a variety of ingredients, was easy to find all over Italy. This recipe, although a little on the sweet side, was one of my favorites.

INGREDIENTS:

1 med-large Butternut Squash
2 Tbsp Olive oil
½ Yellow Onion (chopped)
2 Celery ribs (chopped)
1 cup Risotto Rice (Arborio)
3–4 cups low-sodium Chicken Broth
1 tsp Sea Salt
½ tsp Black Pepper
½ tsp Sage
¼ tsp Nutmeg
¼ tsp Cinnamon
2 Tbsp Butter
¼ cup Parmigiano

DIRECTIONS:

1. Place Squash in a 400-degree oven on a baking sheet for 60 minutes, turning after 30 minutes. When the squash is done it will be soft, and the skin will have begun to turn brown.

2. Cut the squash in half, lengthwise, and let cool. Remove seeds and skin; then cut Squash into large chunks.

3. While squash is cooling, heat Olive Oil in a large sauce pan and cook Onions in it over medium heat for 3–5 minutes.

4. Add Celery and cook for 7–10 minutes, or until the Celery is soft and the Onion begins to brown.

5. Add the Rice and continue to stir for 2–3 minutes; then add 1 cup of Chicken Broth. Add Nutmeg, Sage, Cinnamon, and Salt and Pepper.

6. Once most of broth is absorbed, add the Squash and another cup of broth. Blend all ingredients; then add yet another cup of broth.

7. Cover and cook for another 15–25 minutes, stirring every 5 minutes.

8. When most of the liquid is absorbed* and the rice is tender, add the Butter and Cheese and stir until melted.

9. Serve immediately.

*If mixture seems too dry, add the remaining broth and cook until you get the desired texture.

**Serves 6–8

Hand-Made Pasta

I get just as much joy from making the pasta as I do from eating it. But you have to have both time and patience if you're going to enjoy your pasta-making experience. I also recommend a nice glass of Chianti for the pasta maker.

INGREDIENTS:

1 cup Semolina Flour
2 cups All-Purpose Flour
½ tsp Salt
4 Eggs
2 Egg Yolks
2 Tbsp Olive Oil
½ cup Cold Water

DIRECTIONS:

Making the Pasta dough:

1. Whisk together Semolina Flour, All-Purpose Flour, and Salt. Pour the flour mixture onto a cutting board or counter top; and make a well in the center of it.
2. Beat Egg Yolks in a separate bowl; then pour eggs and Olive Oil into the flour well.
3. Begin to incorporate the Flour mixture into the well. Continue until the well is gone and the dough has a crum-

bly consistency, sprinkling with Cold Water as you go along until you can form a ball.

4. Knead the ball of dough on a lightly floured surface until the dough feels smooth, or about 10 minutes. Add flour if dough seems too wet.

5. Flatten dough into a disk, wrap in plastic wrap, and put in the refrigerator for at least one hour.

Making the Pasta:

1. Separate the dough into 3 or 4 equal parts, to make it easier to manage; especially if using a pasta maker.

2. On a floured work surface, I would then roll out each piece of dough to about ¼ inch thickness, dust with flour; then feed each part through the machine to flatten; and then cut the pasta.

3. If I were cutting by hand, I would roll out the dough into a circle, about the thickness of a penny, 1/16 inch, keeping in mind that when the pasta is boiled it doubles in size.

4. Dust the top with flour; then roll up the pasta circle as you would a sleeping bag.

5. Crosswise—and with a very sharp knife—cut the pasta roll into ⅛- or ¼-inch wide strips. Remember, if the pasta is too perfect no one will believe that you made it by hand.

6. After cutting each pasta circle, separate and unroll them.

7. Allow pasta to dry about 15 minutes before cooking.

Cooking the pasta:

1. Add pasta to a gently boiling pot of salted water until tender.

2. Strain the pasta in a colander, but do not rinse.

3. Serve with your favorite sauce.

* Serves 4 to 6

**When rolling out dough, try rolling in different directions to relax the dough. If the dough continues to shrink as you roll it, cover again with plastic wrap and return to refrigerator for 30 minutes.

***Cover the pasta with whatever suits you; but, as far as I'm concerned, a thick tomato sauce, cooked for hours with meatballs and sausage, can't be beat.

****Wine? Yes, please.

Pasta Di Monteruscello

I learned to cook this dish from a chef at a ristorante near our house in Pozzuoli, Italy; however, I substitute my Grandfather's (we call him Popo) sausage recipe for the chef's original one. The original sausage recipe used only salt and black pepper, whereas my Grandfather's also includes red pepper and fennel. I think the extra heat works well with the sweetness of the cream. Anyway, I think you're going to like this simple recipe. Many great memories were made over this plate of pasta!!

Popo makes the best Italian Sausage

INGREDIENTS:

Sausage

1 lb Ground Pork Butt
½ tsp Black Pepper
½ tsp Red Pepper Flakes
½ tsp Fennel Seeds
1 tsp Salt

*The above ingredients are approximate per taste. I would love to give you the exact family recipe, but I've been sworn to secrecy........sorry.

**You could buy Italian sausage and remove it from the casings, but where would the fun be in that?

Sauce

1 pint Heavy Cream
1 cup Fresh-Grated Parmigiano
½ cup Chopped Walnuts
1 lb Penne Pasta

DIRECTIONS:

1. If you decide to season the pork yourself, mix the Ground Pork and seasonings well—and then mix it some more.

2. Make a small Sausage Patty and fry it. If you are happy with the taste, then move to the next step; otherwise, adjust the ingredients and repeat Step 2.

3. Brown the loose, seasoned Pork; turn down the heat to low and slowly add the Heavy Cream and let simmer for approximately 15 minutes. (Note: Remove some of the grease prior to adding the cream if you'd like.)

4. Boil the water for pasta.

5. Cook the pasta and drain in colander; do not rinse the pasta.

6. Once the sauce starts to thicken, add the Walnuts and Cheese. You should still have a good amount of liquid.

7. Return Pasta to original pot.

8. Combine the Sauce and the Pasta and serve immediately (the pasta will soak up the liquid if it sits too long). Add extra Parmigiano if necessary. Mangia! Mangia!!

*As for a wine, I prefer a Chardonnay. Single Malt Scotch? You might be pleasantly surprised.

Pizza

While living in Naples I got spoiled with great dishes, but none more so than with the pizza. Everything about Neapolitan Pizza was exceptionally great. The crust was chewy, crisp, and, in some spots, charred. The sauce was simple, but full of flavor. The toppings, such as the buffalo mozzarella, were fresh and creamy.

Well, I know that I can't do much about the buffalo mozzarella, unless I want to spent a lot of money to get it, or raise a couple of buffalo, but I can work on replicating the pizza crust.

I've managed to fill the house with smoke, and to almost melt my oven; and I have broken a Pampered Chef cooking stone; all in the attempt to get an area hot enough to cook the pizza like the Neapolitans do. (When the good people at Pampered Chef tell you not to get their cooking stones above a certain temperature, they mean it.)

My last-ditch effort was to put a Cast Iron skillet on my gas grill and CRANK UP THE HEAT! Well, the pizza didn't come out quite like a Neapolitan Pizza. As a matter of fact, the bottom cooked so quickly that it burned. Back to the drawing board.

For now, let's stick with a pizza stone in a 450-degree oven, and the following pizza dough recipes.

Pizza Napoletana at our house on a hot summer's night (about midnight). The round pot (bottom) housed a double crusted pizza with escarole (endive)!!

Below are two recipes that you can use for your pizza dough.

The first one is not really a recipe, but rather a procedure for using frozen dough; while the second one will have you making your own dough if you are willing to spend the time.

Store-Bought Dough

INGREDIENTS:

1 loaf Rhodes White Bread
Olive Oil

DIRECTIONS:

1. Lightly coat the inside of a large bowl with Olive Oil.

2. Place frozen loaf of Rhodes White Bread in bowl and cover bowl with damp towel, after putting a thin coat of Olive Oil on frozen loaf to keep the towel from sticking to it.

3. Allow dough to completely thaw and rise until it has doubled in size. The time will depend upon the temperature of the room.

4. Punch down dough and form into a ball. Return to bowl. Cover and allow to rise again.

5. Heat your *pizza stone for at least 45 minutes in a 450-degree oven.

6. On a lightly floured work surface, using your hands or a rolling pin, form your dough into a circle. While it's cooking, the dough will rise; so flatten your dough according to your desire for a thinner or thicker crust.

7. Place your pizza dough on a lightly floured, or cornmeal-sprinkled, **pizza peel and top with desired toppings.

8. Slide pizza off of pizza peel onto preheated pizza stone and allow to bake for approximately 15 minutes, checking bottom of the pizza for desired crispness.

9. Remove entire pizza stone from oven, understanding that your pizza will continue to cook from the bottom.

10. Slice and enjoy.

*If you don't have a pizza stone and would like to use a cookie sheet or a pizza pan instead, spread dough onto either, after the dough has risen the first time. Once the dough is rolled out onto your cookie sheet or pizza pan, spray lightly with cooking spray and cover with plastic wrap, and allow to rise again; at least 30 more minutes. Add your favorit toppings and bake.

** A pizza peel is a shovel-like tool used to slide pizzas and other baked goods, such as bread and pastries, into, and out of, an oven. Pizza peels are usually made of wood, but can also be made of a combination of wood and thin metal.

Home-Made Dough

(24 hours needed)

INGREDIENTS:

¼ tsp Active Dry Yeast
1 ¼ cups Warm Water
4 cups *"00" Flour or
All-Purpose Flour
2 tsp Fine Sicilian Sea Salt
2 Tbsp Olive Oil

DIRECTIONS:

1. Sprinkle Yeast over water. Yeast should become creamy in 5-10 minutes. If it does not, try another packet of yeast as the previous one was no longer active.
2. Whisk together Flour and Salt in a large bowl.
3. Form a well in the center of the flour.
4. Add Yeast mixture and Olive Oil to the Flour well, then stir until dough mixture comes together.
5. Put dough onto a lightly floured work surface and knead like you mean it for 10 minutes. Put a light coat of oil on

top of dough, cover with a damp dishtowel and let dough, and your arms, rest for 10 minutes.

6. Knead the dough for about 10 more minutes, or until you get the right texture; then form dough into a ball. (**See hint on next page)
7. Place dough into a large, lightly oiled bowl.
8. Cover the bowl tightly with plastic wrap and put in the refrigerator overnight, or for at least 8 hours.
9. Punch down the stiff dough, form a ball by folding the sides over one another. Then tightly cover the bowl with plastic wrap and return to refrigerator for at least 4 hours. (We're getting close!)
10. Remove dough from refrigerator and divide it. Dividing the dough into four pieces will yield four pizzas, each approximately 10 inches in diameter.
11. Shape each piece into a ball and place on a lightly floured work surface. Spray dough with a light coat of water, then loosely cover the dough with a damp towel. Allow to rise until dough has doubled in size (about 2 to 3 hours).
12. On a lightly floured work surface, using your hands or a rolling pin, form your dough into a circle. The dough will rise as it cooks, so flatten your dough according to your desire for a thinner or thicker crust.
13. Place pizza dough on a lightly floured, or cornmeal-dusted, pizza peel and top with desired toppings, such as

your favorite sauce, fresh tomatoes, veggies, etc. I would recommend waiting until approximately the last five minutes of cook-time to add the cheese so that it does not burn.

14. Slide pizza off of pizza peel onto preheated pizza stone, and allow to bake for approximately 15 minutes, checking the bottom of the pizza for desired crispness.

15. Remove entire pizza stone from oven, understanding that your pizza will continue to cook from the bottom.

16. Finally........slice and enjoy!!

* "00" Flour can be purchased at specialty shops or by mail order. This flour makes a pizza dough that is easy to work with, while producing a tender and crispy crust when cooked ; however, Neapolitan pizza has a list of the different required ingredients and other instructions, such as how much time you have to let the dough rest. The "00" flour holds a lot of liquid so Neapolitan-style pizza has a tender crust, but they bake in 50 seconds with a blast of 800-degree heat, so this flour helps maintain the moisture content.

**There is a secret to kneading. If you under knead, the glutens don't hold together and the crust won't have enough texture. If you over-knead you get a hockey puck that won't stretch. It's not a matter of time, but is visual and tactile, an appearance and sense of touch thing. The dough should feel like the texture of memory foam. When you poke the dough and it dents and gently springs back into shape, that's when it's done.

***In Italy they typically drink beer with pizza. I don't discriminate and like to have wine with my pizza sometimes. It's your pizza—drink what you want!!

Sausage & Ricotta Pasta

This recipes will provide you the perfect opportunity to use the fresh ricotta that you have made from the recipe on page 18.

INGREDIENTS:

3 Tbsp Olive Oil
2 cloves Garlic (chopped)
1 lb Italian Sausage (casings removed)
1 can Tomato Sauce (28 oz)
1 ½ cups Water
1 tsp Sugar
2 Bay Leaves
Salt and Black Pepper
1 lb Penne
3 cups Ricotta
½ lb Mozzarella (shredded)
¼ cup Parmigiano

DIRECTIONS:

1. In a deep frying pan, heat Olive Oil and add Garlic, cooking over medium heat about one minute. Add the Sausage and brown.

2. Add Tomato Sauce, Water, Bay Leaves, and Sugar to sausage.

3. Simmer all ingredients for about 30 to 40 minutes, or until the sauce starts to thicken.

4. Once Pasta is cooked and drained, add the pasta to the sauce and mix well.

5. Pour mixture into a baking dish (9″ by 13″, if possible).

6. Put large spoonfuls of the Ricotta on top of the pasta mixture and gently stir some into it, while being careful to leave a few large pockets of ricotta.

7. Cover with Mozzarella and sprinkle with the Parmigiano.

8. Bake uncovered at 400 degrees for approximately 45 minutes or until the cheese on top starts to turn golden.

9. Allow to rest for 15 to 20 minutes before serving.

**Try a Zinfandel with this dish, or, for something different, try a Sicilian Nero d'Avola, one of my new favorites, which is similar to Syrah.*

Spicy Red Sauce (Arrabiata) with Shrimp

The word Arrabiata means "angry" in Italian. You'll find Arrabiata dishes on just about every menu in Naples; however, I didn't have to leave the house to have the following experience.

It was a Tuesday night and I had to be at work early, because we had a five-mile run planned around Capodimonte Park in the middle of Naples. Yup, the Marine Corps is up-and-at-it, even when in Europe.

Around 11 p.m. our door bell (buzzer) woke me up. I saw our land-lord, Giovanni, at the bottom of the stairs waving me down. Curious and concerned, I went to see what was going on. As I walked into his and Lucia's house the aroma of her tomato sauce smacked me right in the face. Sitting around the table were his son Alfonso and friend Antonnio. Apparently they had been out fishing and caught what we would consider langostinos.

So it was at 11 p.m., on a Tuesday night, I was about to be fed a meal to remember. One that lasted until around 3 a.m. After copious amounts of Giovanni's dry white wine. And Limoncello. And espresso. It wasn't like I was going to get sleep anyway.

Luccia put the sweet langostinos atop spaghetti, both covered with a simple, spicy tomato sauce. The result was an unbelievable meal that I will always remember. Lots of stories and laughs made a great meal spectacular. The five-mile run? Not so great.

Antonnio (left) & Giovanni (right): Quite the characters

INGREDIENTS:

1 Tbsp Olive Oil
1 tsp Garlic (crushed)
1 Tbsp Butter
½ cup Dry White Wine
28 oz can Diced Tomatoes (undrained)
2 Tbsp Tomato Paste
½ tsp Red Pepper Flakes
½ tsp Black Pepper
½ tsp Sea Salt
Shrimp (peeled and deveined)
½ Lemon
1 lb Linguine
½ cup fresh Basil leaves

DIRECTIONS:

1. Over medium heat, add Olive Oil and Garlic to a large frying pan and cook for 2 minutes.

2. Add Butter and White Wine and cook for another 3 minutes.

3. Stir in Tomatoes, Tomato Paste, Red and Black Pepper, and Salt, and let simmer for at least 30 minutes, stirring occasionally.

4. While the sauce is cooking, fill a large pot half-way with water and bring to a boil.

5. Add Shrimp to boiling water. Once shrimp turn pink and rise to the surface of the water, remove from heat and drain the water. I like to use a colander.

6. While sauce is cooking and shrimp are cooling, cook your pasta according to its directions.

7. Once shrimp is cool enough to handle, peel the shrimp completely. Once shrimp are peeled, squeeze the juice of the Lemon over them, and set them aside.

8. The sauce should still be thin at this point, but it will be ready for some action. Taste-test to see if it's angry enough for you. If so, pour the sauce into the pot that you cooked the pasta in.

9. Stir the shrimp into the sauce, ensuring the sauce completely coats the shrimp.

10. Stir in the pasta.

11. Serve hot. Garnish with some fresh Basil.

*This dish was really too hot for wine; cold beer would have worked. But I have toned the recipe down a bit so a Riesling works just fine for me.

**Seared Scallops would be a great addition to this dish.

"Great restaurants are, of course, nothing but mouth-brothels. There is no point in going to them if one intends to keep one's belt buckled."

— FREDERIC RAPHAE

CHAPTER FOUR

North Carolina

I have lived in North Carolina for only three years, but during that time there have been plenty of opportunities for memorable gatherings, such as my retirement weekend, and New Year's Eve at the beach. Over the past three years, these occasions have included plenty of great food and fun.

New Year's Day at the beach: Carolina Beach, N.C., 2010

Basil-Lime Butter

We call this our Popcorn Butter, but it's good on many other things, including corn on the cob, potatoes, and other veggies.

INGREDIENTS:

1 stick Salted Butter (softened)
Zest of 2 Limes
Juice of 1 Lime
¼ cup fresh, chopped Basil

DIRECTIONS:

1. Mix together all ingredients. Form butter mixture into a log about the thickness of a quarter with the help of plastic wrap. Refrigerate.
2. To use, simply unwrap the butter and slice off the desired amount.

* For use on salmon, leave out the basil, lime zest and juice, and add soy sauce and pickled ginger.

Cast Iron Skillet Cornbread

This is not a low-cal recipe by any stretch, but I think it is well worth the calories.

INGREDIENTS:

1 tsp Vegetable Oil
4 Tbsp Butter
2 Eggs
1 cup Sour Cream
1 ½ cups Stone-Ground Cornmeal
½ cup Flour
¼ cup Sugar
2 tsp Baking Powder
1 tsp Salt
¼ tsp Baking Soda

DIRECTIONS:

1. Preheat oven to 400 degrees.
2. Rub an 8-inch cast iron skillet with the Oil, then place skillet in oven.
3. Lightly brown the Butter in a small saucepan. Pour browned butter into a mixing bowl.
4. Once butter is cooled, add Eggs and Sour Cream, and whisk well.

5. Combine the Cornmeal, Flour, Sugar, Baking Powder, Salt, and Baking Soda.

6. Combine the dry mix above with the Eggs, Sour Cream, and Butter; and mix until just combined.

7. Pour this batter into the skillet and bake until golden, about 25 minutes.

8. Let the cornbread cool in the skillet for 5 to 10 minutes; then turn onto a wire rack.

9. Slice the cornbread and serve.

Espressotini

Too many of these and you won't know if you are coming or going. Go easy!

INGREDIENTS:

2 oz Espresso
2 ½ oz Vodka
1 oz Kahlua or Godiva Cappucino Liqueur

DIRECTIONS:

1. Make a Double Espresso and let cool to room temperature.
2. Fill cocktail shaker with Ice.
3. Pour Espresso, Vodka, and Kahlua over ice and shake.
4. Pour and serve.

*Line rim of glass with cinnamon and/or cocoa powder.

Fried Pickles

While visiting Nashville's Wildhorse Saloon this summer I discovered fried pickles for the first time. I've seen some pretty ridiculous things being deep fried (think Twinkie), but fried pickles turned out to be exceptionally tasty.

The recipe below was my first attempt at making fried pickles and, although they were not Wildhorse Saloon-great, I can promise that once you eat these tasty little treats, you're gonna experiment with this recipe and make it your own!

INGREDIENTS:

Vegetable Oil
½ cup Pancake Mix
*1/3 cup Club Soda or Stout Beer
¼ tsp Salt
¼ tsp Black Pepper
**Ground Chipotle Pepper
1 cup Flour
Bread & Butter Pickles (Spears or Slices)
Ranch Dressing

DIRECTIONS:

1. Mix the Club Soda or Beer with the Pancake Mix.

2. Add the Salt and both Black and Chipotle Pepper to the Flour; mix thoroughly.

3. Coat Pickles with Flour, and then with the batter.

4. Fry for approximately 3 minutes, or until golden brown.

5. Drain on a paper towel.

6. Serve warm with Ranch Dressing.

*Truth is, you could use Pepsi instead of the Club Soda or Beer if you wanted, just as long as you have carbonation to lighten the batter; but Stout sounds so much sexier.

**Your choice of spices is endless. I liked the heat of the Chipotle Pepper with the sweetness of the Bread & Butter Pickles. Dill Pickles are also a great choice.

***You can make a lot of fried pickles with just a little batter.

****Choice of drink for this dish will depend upon the spices you use, but I don't think you can go wrong with a cold Ale.

Lemon Pasta Salad

This is a great summer-time, barbecue-at-the-beach, near-the-pool favorite.

I poison-tested this on the family last summer and it was a big hit!

INGREDIENTS:

7 Tbsp Olive Oil
2 tsp Lemon Zest
4 Tbsp Fresh Lemon Juice
3 Tbsp Whole Grain Mustard
2 cloves Garlic (minced)
12 ounces Penne, Rotini, or Cellentani Pasta
2 cups Cherry Tomatoes (halved)
1 cup Red Bell Peppers (chopped)
1 ½ cups Feta Cheese (crumbled)
½ cup Green Onions (chopped)
1 cup Kalamata Olives

DIRECTIONS:

1. Whisk Olive Oil, Lemon Juice and Zest, Mustard, and Garlic in small bowl to blend. Season dressing with Salt and Pepper.

2. Cook pasta in large pot of boiling salted water until tender. Drain and allow pasta to cool. Transfer pasta to large bowl.

3. Add Tomatoes, Olives, Bell Peppers, Feta Cheese, and Green Onions.

4. Pour dressing over and toss to coat. Season to taste with Salt and Pepper.

*This gets better, the longer it sits.

Limoncello Shrimp & Spinach

We squeeze lemon on shrimp all the time, right? Well, why not give the shrimp a little sweetness and kick by using Limoncello.

INGREDIENTS:

Handful of Fresh Spinach
½ Tbsp Butter
½ Tbsp Olive Oil
½ Tbsp Garlic (minced)
4 large Shrimp (raw & peeled)
1 to 2 ounces Limoncello
Salt & Pepper

DIRECTIONS:

1. Blanch the Spinach in boiling water for about 30 seconds. Put into bowl of cold water to stop cooking; then squeeze the water out of the spinach and set aside.

2. In a small frying pan, heat Butter and Olive Oil on medium heat.

3. Add Garlic and cook for about 30 seconds.

4. Add Shrimp, cooking for about one minute each side.

5. Drizzle the Limoncello over shrimp while cooking.

6. Pour shrimp over spinach.

7. Salt and Pepper to taste.

8. Serve immediately.

*Works great with scallops, too.

**I'm a big fan of Sauvignon Blanc. If you can find a 2010 Villa Maria, you'll thank me. We refer to it as Love Potion #9.

North Carolina Limoncello

While living in Italy, we were told that the only true LIMONCELLO came from the Isle of Capri, just off the coast of Naples, Italy; everything else was Liquore di Limone. Essentially, it's the same product, but just produced in a different location. There is a debate about its exact origin; but if you make your own, the debate will be over.

This is one of many recipes and, as with any recipe, you can easily make it to your own taste by adjusting the amounts of sugar and the proof of the alcohol you use; however, I wouldn't use alcohol of less than 100 proof.

INGREDIENTS:

2 (750 ml) bottles 190 proof Pure Alcohol (Everclear) or 100 proof Vodka
4 cups Sugar
15 Lemons
1 Lime (optional)
5 cups Water

DIRECTIONS:

1. Peal or zest all Lemons and Lime, leaving behind as much of the white portion as possible as it is bitter.

2. Place lemon and lime zest or skins in a container with the alcohol.

3. Seal container and place in cool, dark place for at least 10 days. The alcohol should now be bright yellow in color.
4. Boil Water. Add the Sugar and stir until dissolved. Let sugar-water cool.
5. Remove peels or zest from alcohol. Add cooled sugar-water to alcohol mix.
6. Mix well and place your Limoncello in a glass bottle, after straining through cheesecloth, if necessary.
7. In a cool and dark place, allow mixture to rest another 10 days (if you can wait).
8. Place in refrigerator or freezer. Limoncello should have a high enough alcohol content that when placed in freezer it will not freeze; however, if it does freeze it will not hurt your masterpeice.

*Should be served cold from refrigerator or freezer.

**Regulate your consumption so as to not end up naked in your pool.

Pasta Primavera with Smoked Salmon

This quick and simple recipe is great to make during a busy week. In the time it takes to cook your pasta, you can have this tasty dish prepared and ready to eat.

I've also made this dish with Hickory Smoked Tuna. StarKist sells this tuna in its Tuna Creations packets; these come in 4.5 oz servings, so I use two of them.

INGREDIENTS:

1 lb Fettucine
3 Tbsp Olive Oil
1 clove Garlic (minced)
½ lb fresh Snow Peas
1 Roasted Red Bell Pepper (cut in strips)
(See recipe p. 33)
1 cup Heavy Cream
8 oz Smoked Salmon
½ cup Parmigiano

DIRECTIONS:

1. Cook Pasta.

2. In a deep frying pan, heat Olive Oil; add Garlic, Snow Peas, and Roasted Pepper, and cook for one minute.

3. Add the Cream and bring to a boil.

4. Add cooked pasta to the above ingredients, along with the Salmon broken into small pieces. Mix.

5. Serve hot with Parmigiano.

*Serves 4

**Chardonnay always works well with salmon.

Pork Chop-A-Lini

INGREDIENTS:

2 Tbsp Olive Oil
½ cup Flour
¼ tsp each, Salt and Pepper
6 Pork Chops (thin cut/pounded thin)
⅓ cup Dry White Wine
5 Tbsp Butter
1 clove Garlic (crushed)
1 package Mushrooms (8 oz sliced)
1 cup low-sodium Chicken Broth
Juice of 2 Lemons
2 Tbsp Capers

DIRECTIONS:

1. Heat Olive Oil in a large sauté pan over medium heat.

2. In a mixing bowl, combine the Flour, Salt, and Pepper.

3. Ensure Pork Chops are no thicker than ¼ inch. Dredge pork chops in flour mixture, shaking off excess.

4. Cook for 1 to 2 minutes per side, browning a bit on each side. Chops should be about 90 percent cooked at this time. Set cooked chops aside while repeating the process until all chops are cooked to 90 percent.

5. Once all chops are cooked, add the White Wine to the pan for deglazing (i.e., removing and dissolving caramelized bits of food from a pan to make a pan sauce).

6. Add Mushrooms, Garlic, and two tablespoons of the Butter.

7. Reduce heat to medium-low.

8. Add Chicken Broth.

9. Add the Lemon Juice and whisk lightly until sauce starts to thicken.

10. Add remaining Butter and Capers, and whisk.

11. Return pork chops to pan and heat for 1 to 2 minutes.

12. Serve hot, with sauce spooned over the chops.

*Serve with mashed potatoes.

**Pinot Grigio or Chardonnay, if you prefer a white wine; while red wine lovers might try a Chianti or a Merlot.

Pumpkin Soup

INGREDIENTS:

1 Tbsp Olive Oil
1 small Onion (diced)
3 cloves Garlic (minced)
½ tsp Cinnamon
½ tsp Cumin
¼ tsp Nutmeg
4 cups Low-Sodium Vegetable Broth
15 oz can Pure Pumpkin
1 Tbsp Chipotle Tabasco
Plain Greek Yogurt
Salt & Pepper

DIRECTIONS:

1. Heat Oil over medium heat; then add Onion and cook until soft.

2. Add Garlic, Cinnamon, Cumin, and Nutmeg, cooking for one minute.

3. Add Vegetable Broth, Pumpkin, and Tabasco. Allow to simmer for at least 30 minutes.

4. I like the soup a little chunky, but puree if you'd like it smooth.

5. Garnish each bowl with a tablespoon of Plain Greek Yogurt, and add Salt and Pepper to taste.

*I prefer a red wine, such as a Zinfandel or Pinot Noir, with this soup; but white wine drinkers may prefer a Riesling. Beer drinkers may try a Pale Ale.

Shuckin' Shack Shrimp

INGREDIENTS:

Shrimp (thawed, shells on)
Olive Oil Cooking Spray
Old Bay Seasoning

DIRECTIONS:

1. Preheat your oven's broiler.

2. Spray cookie sheet with Cooking Spray.

3. In a bowl, sprinkle the desired amount of Old Bay Seasoning on the raw Shrimp, coating both sides of the Shrimp.

4. Spread Shrimp on cookie sheet.

5. Put under broiler for approximately 6 minutes.

6. Serve with Sok's Cocktail Sauce (see page 40) and cold beer.

Special (Veggie) Sauce for Steak

This sauce looks funny, but it smells great and has a big, bold taste. I suppose it would be good on pork, too (chops or sausage). Actually, it's so good that it could make a flip-flop edible.

The fresher the veggies, the better, with this tangy, smokey sauce.

INGREDIENTS:

2 thick Slices Bacon
½ small Onion (quartered)
1 Portobello Mushroom
2 Plum Tomatoes (halved)
Skewer the above and put on grill until bacon and veggies are soft and slightly charred.
4 Prunes (pitted)
3 cloves Garlic
1 Tbsp Chipotle Tabasco
2 Tbsp White Wine Vinegar
2 Tbsp Light Brown Sugar
½ cup Water

DIRECTIONS:

1. 1. Put veggies and all other ingredients, including the bacon, in a blender and blend until you get the desired consistency. I prefer the consistency of a thick tomato sauce. Not hot enough? Add more Tabasco.

2. Pour on your steak, chops, or flip-flop, and enjoy!

**Dark beer or a big red wine will make you a happy camper while you are eating this sauce.

Speculoos

These delicious, spicy cookies, with origins that go back for many centuries, are given to the children in Belgium and France on the Day of St. Nicholas, December 6th; and on December 5th in the Netherlands, where they are called Speculaas. This is a great feast day when the Saint comes to reward the good children and punish the bad! I guess they make the bad kids eat American chocolates; poor things.

In recent decades Speculoos have become available all year round. Dutch and Belgian versions are baked with light-brown beet sugar and baking powder. Spices used in Speculoos are cinnamon, nutmeg, cloves, ginger, cardamon, and white pepper. Most versions are made from white flour, brown sugar, butter, and spices. Some varieties use some almond flour and have slivered almonds embedded in the bottom. Belgian varieties use less or no spice. The dough is stored in a cool place overnight to give the spices time to permeate the dough and add extra flavor. Speculoos dough does not rise much, looking similar to a flat ginger bread. In Belgium, Speculoos are shaped by pressing the dough into decorative wooden molds (of St. Nicholas) rather than using a cutter.

INGREDIENTS:

3 ¼ cups Flour
1 ½ tsp Cinnamon
1 tsp Ground Ginger
1 tsp Cloves
¼ tsp Baking Soda

2 ¼ cups Brown Sugar (packed)
9 Tbsp Butter (softened)
¼ cup Water

DIRECTIONS:

1. Mix Flour, Cinnamon, Ginger, Cloves, and Baking Soda.
2. Beat together Sugar and Butter; and add to flour mixture along with Water.
3. Let the dough rest for 30 minutes.
4. Roll the dough to ¼ inch thickness and cut with a cookie cutter.
5. Place on a greased cookie sheet and bake in a preheated oven (375 degrees) for 10 to 15 minutes.

**Makes approximately two dozen cookies.*

Whipped Sweet Potatoes

This is a quick and easy way to add something special to your sweet potatoes.

INGREDIENTS:

2 medium Sweet Potatoes
½ cup Heavy Cream
2 Tbsp Butter
1 Vanilla Bean
Salt & Pepper

DIRECTIONS:

1. Clean the Sweet Potatoes.
2. Poke holes in sweet potatoes or scrape skin.
3. Run potatoes under water and wrap each in a paper towel, ensuring each potato is completely covered.
4. Microwave for approximately 11 minutes or until potatoes are soft to the touch. (If you have the time, bake the potatoes, without the paper towel, for approximately 30 minutes in a 400-degree oven.)
5. While potatoes are cooling, put the Cream, Butter and Vanilla Bean, seeds removed, in a small sauce pan. Bring all ingredients to a simmer.

6. Once potatoes are cool enough to handle, cut them in half and remove skin.
7. Transfer potatoes to a food processor, or bowl for using a hand mixer, to get potatoes smooth.
8. Remove the vanilla bean from the sauce, then add the sauce to the potatoes, processing or mixing until smooth.
9. Add Salt and Pepper to taste, and serve.

"The only time to eat diet food is while you're waiting for the steak to cook."

—JULIA CHILD

CHAPTER FIVE

Christmas

Some of my best memories of Hawai'i are from Christmas. Yes, Santa coming ashore on a canoe is cool, but that's not what I'm referring to.

Dinner at our house became a tradition among our friends. I'd like to think that it was my charming personality and boyish good looks, but I'm pretty sure that it was the food: Manicotti. Meatballs. Sausage. Leg of lamb. Dare I say.......Carrot Cake?

The food list went on and on, as did the wine list. The record number of friends joining us for Christmas dinner was seventeen. We kept adding tables, starting in the dining room, through the living room, onto the deck, until we had enough seats for everyone to sit, as a family, and eat at one time. Those were special days, with special friends.

This last chapter of Sex & Spaghetti *is all about that meal and the recipes that were part of it.......plus a few extra ones for kicks.*

Kaneohe Christmas, 2007

Anna's Italian Wedding Soup

My brother makes a great pot of soup. And although he has stated that the recipe below is complete, I have reason to believe that he may be holding back an ingredient or two. Either way, I think you're gonna like this hearty, tasty soup.

INGREDIENTS:

1 Roasted or Boiled Chicken
(rostissierre chicken works great)
1 lb Sicilian Meatballs (marble size)
6 cans Low-Sodium Chicken Broth (12 oz)
2 pkgs Fresh Spinach (chopped)
Carrots (chopped)
Celery (chopped)
1 lb Pastina
Salt & Pepper
Parmigiano

DIRECTIONS:

1. Blanch the Spinach for 2 minutes; then discard the water, as it will be bitter.

2. If using a fresh Chicken, boil the chicken until cooked; then discard this water also. Chop the Chicken into bite-sized chunks.

3. Fill a large soup pot with the Chicken Broth, Spinach, Chicken, Carrots, and Celery and bring to slow boil.

4. Make the Meatballs. (See Sicilian Meatball recipe on p. 35). Once the meatballs are cooked, add them to soup.

5. Bring to a boil, reduce heat, and simmer for at least 4 hours.

6. When ready to eat, stir in the Pastina and allow it to cook according to the directions on the package.

7. Serve hot, adding some Salt, Pepper, and Parmigiano to taste.

You have to do something while the soup is cooking!

Leg of Lamb

INGREDIENTS:

1 Leg of Lamb (deboned)
2 cloves Garlic (quartered)
4 Bay Leaves
and/or
Rosemarry Sprigs
Salt
Black Pepper

DIRECTIONS:

1. Prepare the rotisserie on your grill. Preheat grill to 450 degrees.

2. Take a paring knife and make a hole in the lamb, big enough and deep enough, so that your index finger can fit in it.

3. Stuff a piece of garlic, a piece of bay leaf or rosemary, and as much Salt and Black Pepper as you can fit, into the hole that you cut.

4. Repeat this process until all ingredients are gone; add more if you like.

5. Ensure that the leg of lamb is secure on your rotisserie.

6. Put a small pan of water on the inside of your grill to keep the moisture level up.

7. Cook lamb for approximately 15 minutes on 450 degrees, and then lower to 325 degrees.

8. A five-pound leg should take approximately 2 hours to cook, but use a meat thermometer to verify that it's reached the temperature you desire.

*Enjoy with a 2010 Yalumba Shiraz, or just about any Shiraz from Australia's Barossa Valley.

**Many people enjoy Mint Jelly with their Lamb, but our family was always partial to my Grandpa's canned Banana Peppers. Since you won't be able to get your hands on those, buy some hot banana peppers and do the following: In a blender, blend peppers, garlic, onion, lemon juice, salt, sugar and olive oil to the desired consistency. How much of each ingredient? Well, as much as you like!

Lemon Ricotta Cookies

This was my Grandma Notareschi's recipe (we called her Momo). Once again I have taken the liberty of experimenting with her recipe. These are a big hit at Christmas.

INGREDIENTS:

Cookie Dough

2 cups Sugar
1 cup Butter (melted)
3 Eggs
2 tsp Vanilla
1 tsp *Lemon Oil (or more to taste)
1 tsp Baking Powder
1 tsp Salt
4 cups Flour
15 oz Ricotta

DIRECTIONS:

1. Blend the above ingredients, minus the Flour and Ricotta, by hand.
2. Add Flour and Ricotta and mix.
3. Form dough into the size of golf balls. I use a small ice cream scoop. Place dough on cookie sheet and flatten to about ¼ inch.

4. Bake @ 350 for about 12 to 14 minutes.

**Makes about 4 dozen cookies.

ICING

3 Tbsp Milk
½ tsp Lemon Oil (more/less to taste)
2 cups Powered Sugar
Food coloring (your favorite color)

1. Mix all Icing ingredients, adding more sugar or milk as necessary to get the right consistency for spreading.

*Lemon Oil is different from Lemon Extract in that the extract will contain alcohol. Use Lemon Oil as you would lemon zest, with ¼ teaspoon of the oil being the approximate equivalent of 1 tablespoon grated rind.

Many of the Christmas cookies and desserts, including the Lemon Ricotta and Cuccidati, that we enjoyed.

Mar's Manicotti

My Mom makes the best manicotti! These little cheese-filled bundles of goodness have been fought over at more family gatherings than I can remember.

INGREDIENTS:

Crepes

1 cup Flour
2 Eggs
½ cup Water
½ cup Milk
¼ tsp Salt
2 Tbsp Butter (melted)

DIRECTIONS:

1. Mix all ingredients well. Consistency should be that of heavy cream.
2. Heat a small (8-inch), non-stick frying pan over medium-high heat.
3. Pour a few tablespoons of batter onto the center of the pan. Remove the pan from heat and swirl the pan so that the batter makes a very thin coating. Return to heat.
4. Once the ends start to curl and the batter looses its shine, turn the crepe over using a spatula or your fingers (or get fancy and try flipping it in the air).

5. Once flipped, the crepe should be completely cooked in about 30 seconds.

6. Crepes can be stacked.

FILLING

32 oz Ricotta
1 tsp Parsley, chopped
2 Eggs
½ tsp Salt

1. Mix all filling ingredients well. I like to use a small wooden spoon or heavy whisk.

2. Because I make my crepes on the small side, I take one tablespoon of the cheese filling, place it in the middle of the crepe, and then fold the crepe around the filling to form a manicotti.

3. Put a thin layer of Nicky's Pasta Sauce (see recipe on page 28) in the bottom of the baking dish prior to lining up the manicotti, side by side. Once the dish is filled, cover the manicotti with another thin layer of sauce.

4. Seal the dish by covering it with foil. Bake at 350 for 45 min. If you can wait, allow to cool a bit, about 20 minutes, before trying to serve. Add the desired amount of sauce and sprinkle on some Parmigiano for good measure.

*Because of the rich sauce that I recommend using for this dish, my favorite wine would be any Italian red.

Rosie's Cuccidati

There's a long story behind this Bartlone family recipe. Like to hear it? Here it goes:

My Grandma Bartlone was a great cook who had many signature dishes, but a few years ago something reminded me of these fig cookies that she used to make at Christmas. So I asked around the family and found that one of my uncles had the recipe. I wrote down the recipe, gathered the ingredients, and set out to re-create one of my Grandma's many masterpieces.

I meticulously followed the recipe, not wanting to forget anything, and was pretty happy with the final results. I brought a few dozen cookies to a family gathering, where we all agreed that we had missed these cookies, and that they were good, but that something was missing.

So the next time I talked with my uncle, we were discussing the cookies, saying that maybe it was impossible to re-create that exact taste. This is the point in the conversation when he asked, "What kind of whiskey did you use?" And I said, "Whiskey? What whiskey? You didn't tell me about whiskey! What else is supposed to be in this recipe?" We've been laughing about that conversation every since!

I am happy to report that every time I make these cookies, they get just a little closer to tasting the way that they should. Practice, and the correct ingredients, make perfect.

FILLING

12 oz Figs (soak in warm water to soften)

6 oz Raisins (soak also)
1 cup Almonds (toasted and ground)
1 Tbsp Cinnamon
1 Tbsp Vanilla
4 Tbsp Honey
Zest and juice of 2 large Oranges
½ tsp Black Pepper
½ tsp Salt
2 shots Whiskey

FILLING DIRECTIONS:

1. Mix all ingredients; then grind in a meat grinder. Mix again. Cover and put in refrigerator overnight.

DOUGH

1 Egg
1 cup Sugar
½ cup Crisco (melted)
⅛ tsp Salt
½ cup Sour Milk (see p. 157)
1 tsp Vanilla Extract
1 tsp Lemon Zest
4 cups Flour
½ tsp Baking Powder
½ tsp Baking Soda

1. Whisk Egg, Sugar, and Crisco.
2. Add Salt, Sour Milk, Vanilla Extract, and Lemon Zest to the above and mix well.
3. Combine Flour, Baking Powder, and Baking Soda. Sift into above ingredients. Put in refrigerator for 30 minutes.

4. It's easy to overwork this dough—I've learned the hard way. Once baked, the cookies should be light and fluffy.

5. I've seen these cookies made in different shapes, including rolled into a small log; but I use a round cutter that's about 2 inches across, after I use a rolling pin to roll out the dough to about the thickness of a nickel.

6. Spoon filling onto cut-out dough, and fold the dough over to make a crescent moon shape. Pinch edges.

7. Bake at 350 for 10 to 12 minutes or until brown on bottom.

***Makes about 4 dozen cookies.*

ICING

1 Tbsp Milk
2 drops Almond Extract (or try Orange or Lemon)
2 cups Powered Sugar
Food coloring (your favorite color)

1. Mix all Icing ingredients, adding more sugar or milk as necessary to get the right consistency. Drizzle over fresh Cuccidati.

Stuffed Artichokes

I grew this artichoke right here in N.C.

INGREDIENTS:

4 Artichokes
1 cup Olive Oil
8 oz Mushrooms (sliced)
2 cloves Garlic (minced)
½ medium White Onion (chopped)
½ cup Pine Nuts (toasted)
3 cups Italian Bread Crumbs (VIGO or Progresso Brands)

DIRECTIONS:

1. Heat oven to 350. On a cookie sheet toast Pine Nuts for approximately 5 minutes. Do not let burn.

2. In a medium frying pan, heat 1 Tablespoon of the Olive Oil over medium heat; then add Mushrooms, Garlic, and Onion. Cook for 5 minutes.

3. In a food processor, put the ingredients from frying pan and the Pine Nuts, adding a little of the Olive Oil to assist in combining these ingredients.

4. Slowly add the Bread Crumbs and more Olive Oil to the food processor. The final product should be a dry mixture. Put this mixture in a large bowl.

5. Prepare Artichokes by removing stems, so that Artichoke sits upright. To assist in stuffing the Artichokes, take each one and slam the base of it against your counter top to loosen the leaves.

6. Put an Artichoke into the bowl and fill the Artichoke with the mixture, stuffing each leaf about half-full.

7. Once all Artichokes are stuffed, arrange in a large pot so that each one will stay upright and not fall over; it's okay if they touch—they like each other.

8. Add water to the pot so that it raises about 1 inch on the Artichokes. Drizzle artichokes with olive oil. Cover and steam for 4 to 5 hours, adding water as needed so as to not burn the bottom of the Artichokes.

9. After 4 hours remove an Artichoke leaf to check for tenderness. If tender, try not to eat the entire thing before dinner.

10. Serve Warm

Stuffed Mushrooms

INGREDIENTS:

1 cup Whole Mushrooms
¼ cup Olive Oil
4 Tbsp Butter
½ tsp Garlic (minced)
¼ cup Italian Breadcrumbs (VIGO or Progresso Brands)
¼ cup Parmigiano Cheese

DIRECTIONS:

1. Preheat oven to 350 degrees.
2. Remove stems from Mushrooms and chop stems in half.
3. Heat 1 teaspoon of the Olive Oil and sauté Garlic for one minute.
4. Add Mushroom Stems and Butter, and sauté until stems are soft, about 5 to 8 minutes.
5. In a food processor, combine all ingredients: Mushroom stems, Garlic, Breadcrumbs, Cheese, and remaining Olive Oil, to make the mushroom stuffing.
6. Pulse to reach desired consistency, adding more Olive Oil if Mushroom Stuffing is too dry.

7. Use a teaspoonful of Mushroom Stuffing to fill each Mushroom Cap.

8. Place Stuffed Mushrooms on non-stick baking sheet and bake for 15 to 18 minutes, or until the Mushrooms are tender.

9. Let cool slightly and serve.

*The above ingredients should be enough to fill approximately 20 Mushrooms.

"I cook with wine, sometimes I even add it to the food."

—W.C. Fields

CONCLUSION

Digestivo e Caffé

I hope you've enjoyed Sex & Spaghetti *and have made some fond memories while experimenting with its recipes.*

In Italy, the digestivo, if it is served after the coffee, is the drink that concludes the meal. Grappa, Amaro, Limoncello, or other alcoholic fruit or herbal drinks are consumed with the intent of easing digestion.

Since this is the conclusion of Sex & Spaghetti, *and since you've actually read this far, I think we both need a drink.*

Saluté!!

Three generations of trouble: (from left) Uncle Ed, Popo and yours truly.

"It's all about the food and the wine and the things that go BUMP in the night."

—N. Bartlone

Glossary

Allspice *– Ground from a pea-sized berry from the evergreen pimiento tree. The name allspice comes from the fact that the flavor tastes like a combination of nutmeg, cinnamon, and cloves.*

Almonds *– One of the most nutritious of all nuts, containing more magnesium than oatmeal or even spinach. Toasted, sliced, ground, or made into milk or oil, the almond is very versatile and has been used in many dishes throughout the world.*

Andouille Sausage *– A smoked sausage made from ground pork and garlic, seasoned with salt and black pepper, and stuffed into a sausage casing that is usually made from beef or pork. The sausage is smoked over pecan wood and sugar cane for up to 14 hours. Andouille is an intensely flavored, spicy sausage with a dark color, and in the U.S. it is mostly associated with Cajun cuisine.*

Anise Seeds – *Sweet and aromatic, with a licorice-like flavor. The seeds, whole or ground, are used in a wide variety of regional and ethnic confections, including the black jelly bean and the Italian cookie, pizzelle.*

Artichokes – *One of the oldest foods know to humans; a perennial in the thistle group of the sunflower family, believed to be a native of the Mediterranean. In full growth, the plant spreads to cover an area about six feet in diameter and reaches a height of three to four feet. The 'vegetable' that we eat is actually the plant' s flower bud.*

Balsamic Vinegar – *A dark-red vinegar made from the unfermented juice of pressed grapes, aged in wooden casks. Trebbiano, a white grape, is most commonly used. The most authentic Balsamic is produced around Modena in Northern Italy. Balsamic Vinegar tastes sweet with a slightly sour edge.*

Basil – *An herb with a flavor that is between clove and licorice. Dried basil is more mild than fresh basil, but is still excellent in sauces and sprinkled on salads.*

Bay Leaves – *The dried leaf of the Bay Laurel tree, which is grown all over the Mediterranean. There are two main types of bay leaf: The Mediterranean bay leaf, which is widely used in Mediterranean cooking; and the Californian bay leaf, which is much stronger in flavor. Bay leaves are never eaten, but are used to add extra flavour to a number of dishes.*

Capers – *The immature buds plucked from a small bush native to the Middle East and Mediterranean regions of the world. Fresh caper blossoms are not especially flavorful, but their sharpness increases after they are sun-dried and brined in vinegar. Capers have an intense flavor, so* *most recipes only require a few to add sharpness; a distinctive ingredient in Italian cuisine, especially in Sicily. Commonly used in salads, pizzas, and pasta sauces. Capers are also known for being one of the ingredients of tartar sauce. They are often served with cold smoked salmon.*

Cardamom – *A spice made from the seed pods of various plants in the ginger family. Cardamom has a strong, pungent flavor and aroma, with hints of lemon, mint, and smoke.*
The two main types are black cardamom and green cardamom. Cardamom is used mainly in Indian and Middle Eastern cuisine.

Cayenne Pepper – *A hot, pungent powder made from the cayenne chile. Cayenne chiles are generally sold dried and used in soups and sauces. Used both in cooking and medicine, it owes its hot flavor to a chemical called capsicum.*

Cilantro – *An herb with a pungent odor sometimes called Mexican Parsley; commonly found in Mexican dishes and salsas. It is related to coriander, the ground seed of the leafy cilantro plant.*

Cloves – *A flower bud from an aromatic evergreen tree that grows in the tropics of Asia and South America. The bud and stem are ground and used as a spice, or in certain cigarettes or incense. Clove is used sparingly in dishes as it has an extremely strong flavor.*

Coconut Milk – *The liquid that comes from the grated meat of a coconut. The color and rich taste of the milk can be attributed to the high oil content. Coconut milk is used as the base for many curry recipes.*

Cornstarch *– Finely ground corn flour, used as a thickener in cooking. Also mixed with sugar to make powdered sugar.*

Crisco *– A brand of shortening made entirely of vegetable oil.*

Cumin *– A flowering plant that has been grown as a spice since ancient times, native to the eastern Mediterranean region and eastern India. Cumin has a distinctive aroma that compliments the natural sweetness of a food. Cumin is most frequently used in Indian and Mexican cuisine. It is used in curry powder and is the source of a distinct odor that emanates from the skin of people who routinely eat foods prepared with cumin.*

Fennel Seed *– The slightly sweet, licorice-flavored seed of the fennel plant, often used to season Italian sausage and pasta sauces.*

Feta Cheese *– A cured Greek cheese traditionally made from sheep or goat's milk. This soft and crumbly cheese has a salty, tangy flavor; perfect for pasta salads.*

Fig *– A soft pear-shaped fruit with sweet dark flesh and many small seeds; may be eaten fresh or dried. High in calcium and fiber, they have a laxative effect and contain many antioxidants.*

Five-Spice Powder *– Important in Chinese cooking; usually consists of cinnamon, star anise, cloves, fennel, and Szechwan peppercorns.*

Ginger (fresh and powdered) *– A pungent, spicy rhizome having a lot of nutrition packed into it, making it good for the blood and for* *gastrointestinal functions.* ***Tumeric*** *and* ***Cardamom*** *are also part of this family. Young ginger is used for pickling or sliced thin and used to stir-fry. The older, more fibrous ginger is better for flavoring. Powdered dry ginger root is typically used as a flavoring for recipes such as gingerbread, crackers, cakes, ginger ale, and ginger beer.*

Horseradish – *A root vegetable native to Russia or Hungary and unrelated to radishes. Horseradish is most widely used as a condiment and as an ingredient in sauces and dressings. The mustard-like oil in horseradish is what brings tears to your eyes.*

Lemon Oil – *An essential oil that is extracted from lemon peels. Used sparingly in dishes because it has an intense flavor.*

Lemon Zest – *The zest is the colorful outer layer of the citrus peel; desirable because it contains essential oils that give a strong, pleasant flavor, whereas the pith – the white part of the peel – has a very bitter flavor.*

Liquid Smoke – Consists of smoke produced through the controlled burning of wood chips or sawdust, and then condensed into a solid or liquid form, and then dissolved in water.

Mozzarella – *A cheese originally made from water-buffalo's milk (and still is in Naples, Italy), but now made from cow's milk. Mozzarella is soft and mild tasting. Great in baked pasta dishes and, everyone's favorite, on a pizza.*

Old Bay Seasoning – *A brand of spice mix popular in and on seafood dishes, corn on the cob, and french fries, to name a few.*

Oregano – *A member of the mint family, with a bitter flavor; an essential part of many Mediterranean dishes. Dried oregano is more potent than are the fresh green leaves.*

Oyster Sauce – *A salty brown sauce made from salted oysters, water, soy, and cornstarch; typically used in Asian dishes.*

Parmigiano (Parmesan in English) – *A richly nutty and sweet flavored cheese; geniune Parmigiano-Reggiano cheese is produced in the Emilia-Romagna region of Italy. Best freshly grated into or onto hot ingredients such as sauces and pasta. The rind is sometimes used to flavor soups and sauces.*

Parsley – *The mild curly variety of this popular herb is most often used as a garnish; the flat-leafed Italian variety used mostly for seasoning has a stronger flavor.*

Pastina – *Typically used in Italian cuisine: the smallest of the pasta products. It is made from wheat flour and may include egg. Often used in dishes made for children.*

Pecorino Cheese – *A hard Italian cheese made from ewe's milk.*

Pine Nuts – *Also called pignoli; famous for their role in the Italian basil sauce known as Pesto. Toasting the pine nuts produces the most flavor.*

Prunes – *Dried plums.*

Rosemary – *An herb with needle-shaped leaves that have a piny flavor. The dried or ground leaves retain their strong flavor and should be used sparingly.*

Sage – *An herb used in savory dishes with pork or sausage and as a flavoring in biscuits and cornbread; one of the ingredients used in poultry seasoning. Its strong smell is often used to mask the aroma of stronger flavored meats such as goose and duck. Whether fresh or dried, use sparingly as it has a very strong flavor.*

Sazon Goya – *A brand of Spanish seasoning containing coriander seed (cilantro) and annatto (achiote). Used to flavor meats, chicken, fish,vegetables, soups and sauces.*

Semolina Flour – *Durum wheat that has been ground into flour.*

Sour Milk – *When left to sit, the bacteria in milk will eventually cause it to sour. Warmer temperatures will make the milk sour faster. Add 1 tablespoon of lemon juice or vinegar to one cup of milk to make your own sour milk. Let sit for 15 minutes.*

Soy Sauce (Shoyu) – *Often used in stir-fried dishes for its robust flavor, soy sauce is made from fermented soybeans and wheat barley. 'Shoyu' is the Japanese word for soy sauce.*

Texas Pete – *A specific brand of Hot Sauce using a secret blend of three different types of peppers.*

Thyme – *A gray-green versatile herb with flavors of pine, mint, and lemon, with a subtle aroma. Thyme works well with fish, poultry, soups, lamb, eggs, vegetables, and more.*

Tomato Paste – *Tomatoes that have been cooked for several hours and reduced to a thick, red concentrate before being strained. It is sold in* *cans and tubes. Can be used for thickening sauces or as the base for ketchup.*

Watercress – *A hardy perennial herb which can be put in sandwiches to add a little spark; steamed and eaten as a side dish; or added to soups. This peppery, delicate, dark-green leafy vegetable, that grows wild in cool streams of running water, was prescribed for his patients by Hippocrates; and was eaten by Romans emperors, who may have expected it to cure baldness.*

Worcestershire Sauce – *Originally bottled in Worcester, England; a fermented flavoring that is matured for several months in oak barrels. It contains malt vinegar, molasses, corn syrup, anchovies, onions, salt, garlic, tamarind, cloves, and chili pepper extract. Worcestershire sauce is added to salad dressings, gravies, and Bloody Mary cocktails.*

Marine Corps Retirement, 2011

18161512R00100

Made in the USA
Charleston, SC
20 March 2013